babycakes

babycakes

VEGAN, GLUTEN-FREE, AND (MOSTLY) SUGAR-FREE RECIPES FROM NEW YORK'S MOST TALKED-ABOUT BAKERY

Erin McKenna

WITH CHRIS CECHIN
PHOTOGRAPHS BY TARA DONNE

Clarkson Potter/Publishers
New York

Published in the United States by Clarkson
Potter/Publishers, an imprint of the Crown
Publishing Group, a division of Random House,
Inc., New York.
www.crownpublishing.com
www.clarksonpotter.com

CLARKSON POTTER is a trademark and POTTER
with colophon is a registered trademark of
Random House, Inc.

Library of Congress Cataloging-in-
Publication Data
McKenna, Erin, 1976–
    Babycakes : vegan, gluten-free and (mostly)
sugar-free recipes from New York's most talked-
about bakery / Erin McKenna. — 1st ed.
       p.   c.m.
    Includes index.
    1. Gluten-free diet—Recipes.   2. Celiac
disease—Diet therapy—Recipes.   3. Food
allergy—Diet therapy.   4. BabyCakes (Bakery).
I. Title.
RM237.86.M38   2009
641.5′638—dc22   2008025462

ISBN 978-0-307-40883-9

Printed in China

Design by Laura Palese

Photograph on page 56 copyright © 2009 by
Marcelo Krasilcic

10 9 8 7 6 5 4 3 2

First Edition

This book is dedicated to my mother, Mary, and my father, Frank. Without their sterling examples, I would never have been confident enough to take the risk, had the faith to know I could make it a success, or have the ethics required to keep the bakery alive.

Thank you. I love you both so, so much.

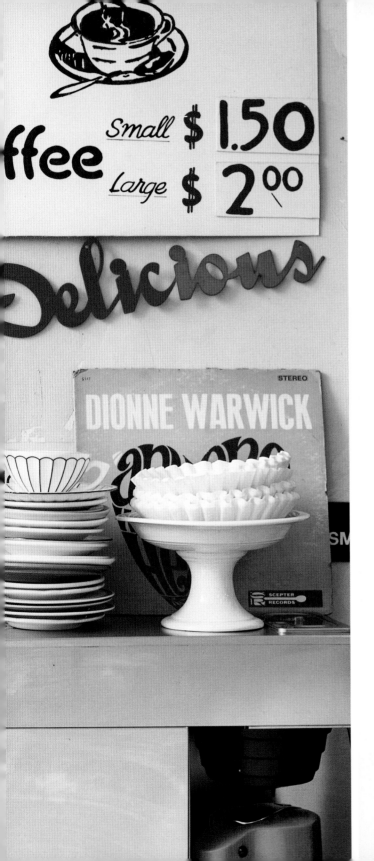

contents

foreword

A couple years ago I was invited on a tour bus with Jerry Lee Lewis. Typically I show my appreciation for this sort of thing by bringing treats from Craft, but the friend who had arranged the outing suffers from celiac disease, limiting us to snacks made without wheat or gluten. Frankly, I was stumped. My wife had read about BabyCakes and stopped by to load up on cupcakes and brownies for the tour bus. To my surprise, the treats went over like great balls of fire.

Soon after I was asked by *Inc.* magazine to work with Erin for their annual mentoring issue. Though I needed no persuading, Erin sent the mother-of-all-care-packages to my office. Now, my staff is a finicky and jaded bunch, used to treats loaded with butter, eggs, and refined sugar. In our world, vegan is pejorative.

Not this time.

My staff hoovered everything up, leaving nothing but crumbs (if that) for me.

When I visited BabyCakes, I was impressed at the line of people waiting to get in. Could there be that many celiacs in New York City? As the customers filed through, I realized: most were not. Alongside those with allergies or food sensitivities were the usual mix of demanding New Yorkers needing a cupcake fix, and this tchotchke-filled, postage-stamp of a shop was their bakery of choice. Healthfulness was beside the point.

In this book, Erin has finally shared her trade secrets—the ingredients and techniques that lend BabyCakes' desserts the flavors, textures, and happiness-factor you'd find in the best patisserie. The highest praise I can offer is this: follow her recipes to the letter and you'll fool them every time.

—Tom Colicchio

introduction

●○●○●○●○●○●○●○●○●○●○●○●○●○●○

i am not a baker by training, but I am without a doubt a competition-level snacker. When I was diagnosed with wheat and dairy allergies in 2004, though, I was forced to face an uncertain future of curtailed nibbling. Braced for the worst, I scoured upscale health-food markets for snacks that met my finicky standards and found that allergy-conscious shoppers faced a wasteland of uninspired products made from baffling, inaccessible ingredients. It seemed a real possibility that my days of midday indulgences and nightly sweets were all behind me, a thought more frightening than photographs of my eighth-grade perm!

Yet I couldn't be alone in this. Surely there were others out there just like me, and beyond them an even larger group looking for an attractive alternative to overly sweet, overly fattening, unimaginably bad-for-you desserts. I decided to take matters into my own hands. Confined to my tiny Brooklyn apartment's kitchen, I spent more than a year developing a bakery's worth of sweet and savory bits. A million recipe attempts and a thousand mental meltdowns later, I was set to open my bakery, BabyCakes NYC.

○●○●○●○●○●○●○●○●○●○●○●○●○●○●

When a boy takes the last piece of bread from the plate, he'll have to kiss the cook ...

Four days prior to the bakery's opening, *Time Out New York* ran a story introducing us to Manhattan's Lower East Side. By ten o'clock the following morning, a line of customers had formed outside the bakery, not knowing that my oven had not yet been delivered. People were peeking in and tapping impatiently on the window while I hid in the back, brushing my hair nervously. One elderly woman eventually forced her way inside and subjected me to an impassioned account of walking two hours from her home on the Upper West Side only to find she'd been cruelly misled. Aghast, embarrassed, and paralyzingly fragile, I quickly teared up, and soon it was she who was consoling me! Others, noticing my distress, left more peacefully, disappointed but promising to return.

Of course, we eventually did open for business, in August 2005, and have been blessed ever since with a loyal and far-reaching clientele. I've long since lost track of the number of allergic children and parents who have made the pilgrimage from San Francisco or Austin or Honolulu to my bakery for their child's first cupcake, but it's fair to say that teary-eyed exchanges between me and such parents are a weekly (and borderline embarrassing) occurrence. There's also no way to quantify how many people without food constraints have lent me their support and become regular customers—based purely on the taste of our products.

I do not consider myself timid in the kitchen, and I strongly encourage you to replace any nervousness with courage. On these pages are hundreds of the baking secrets I've learned and developed. You will most certainly find plenty to keep you entertained: brownies and cookies, muffins and teacakes, biscuits and scones, pies and cobblers . . . the holy and glorious cupcake. Along the way I'll help you navigate the potholes and pitfalls of alternative baking, providing you with tips and guidelines that ensure success. I've tried to be specific, and in most cases it is important that you follow my instructions carefully. Ultimately, though, I hope you'll feel empowered to take control of a fresh list of ingredients—that rather than the pantry's subjecting you to its will, you dictate your own exciting outcomes.

Remember: It is important never to be discouraged. Sure, you'll botch a batch on occasion, and a few of your pennies will no doubt be donated to Lord Garbage. But if I've learned anything, it's that mistakes only make success all the more delicious.

Five years into this adventure, I'm very proud to finally present you with *BabyCakes.* I promise you, it is like no recipe book you've used before.

Let's get busy!

○ ○

tools, ingredients, & tips

A cursory flip through these recipes reveals several ingredients that may be new to you, as well as some techniques that differ from those used in conventional baking books. This section contains information about these alternative ingredients and other pointers that will help you get the best possible results.

It is important to note that while *all* of the recipes are vegan, not all are gluten-free and/or sugar-free. If you have concerns about gluten, please read "Spelt Versus Gluten-Free," page 23, and review the list of ingredients carefully before you begin any recipe.

I've learned countless things the hard way over the course of developing these recipes, and I'd like to help you avoid following in my messy footsteps. All cooking involves a learning process, but I promise that with every recipe and each mistake, things *will* get easier.

Every time you bake from this book, follow these three simple rules:

1. Read the recipe all the way through.

2. Identify and prepare necessary ingredients.

3. Be precise. Follow instructions as closely as possible.

○ ○

TOOLS OF THE TRADE

Here's a bare-bones list of kitchen must-haves.

Cutting board: Both plastic and wooden cutting boards work well, but choose one with a sizable surface area.

Whisk: For mixing together dry ingredients and making smooth batters—you'll use one for every recipe in this book.

Rubber spatula: For folding together ingredients as well as collecting all available batter from your mixing bowl, thereby avoiding waste. It is absolutely essential.

Frosting spatula: Sometimes referred to as a *palette knife,* this spreads frosting evenly across the surfaces of cakes and cupcakes.

Measuring spoons: Invest in a set of spoons ranging from ⅛ teaspoon to 1 tablespoon.

Measuring cups: In this cookbook, all ingredients, including liquids, are measured in a dry measure. Dry-ingredient measuring cups are usually metal, hold a precise quantity, and have a flat handle. You will need a set ranging from ¼ to 1 cup. (See "Measurements," page 22.)

Mixing bowls, small and medium: Whatever your preference—metal, plastic, glass—it is important to have at least two bowls, preferably of different sizes.

Zester: For paring lemon and other citrus peels.

Potato peeler, grater, sharp knives, food processor, or blender: Those vegetables aren't going to chop themselves, but I'll leave it to you to decide which tool is most effective. At the bakery, we alternate between high- and low-tech tools, as each has its pros and cons. Proceed according to your particular mood or fancy.

Pastry brush: For oiling mini-muffin trays and loaf pans and for brushing dough.

Rolling pin: Get yourself a wooden one, with or without handles. You will use it in preparing pie and biscuit recipes.

Stainless-steel dough scraper: Also known as a *bench scraper,* this tool comes in handy when ridding prep surfaces of unwanted dough or transferring chopped ingredients to a bowl.

Ice cream scoop/melon baller: Thumb-release scoops are the most effective tool for achieving uniform measures for cookies, cupcakes, and muffins. I use a ¼-cup ice cream scoop for cupcakes and a 1-inch melon baller for cookies.

Plastic squeeze bottle: Any simple variety helps in filling brownies and drizzling sauces over crumb cakes (pages 110–113).

Cookie cutter: Used for portion control and uniformity in items like biscuits and scones.

Cupcake liners: Available at most grocery stores, these prevent cupcakes from sticking to the pan.

Cupcake, muffin, and mini-muffin tins: Muffin cups are slightly larger than cupcake cups, by about 1 inch in diameter. Because these vary in size, try to get the correct one for each recipe to ensure accurate baking times.

Parchment paper: Because some of the ingredients used in our recipes are stickier than their conventional counterparts, we recommend lining all baking sheets. Wax paper is not an adequate substitute.

Wire cooling rack: This raised rack allows for baked goods to cool properly.

Baking sheets/pie pans: Any type will suffice; each will be used often.

Loaf pans (7 x 4 x 3 inches): Stock up on more than one—before long, you'll be baking for the entire neighborhood.

INGREDIENTS

(Please refer also to "Resources," page 139, and "Purveyors," page 140).

Bob's Red Mill Gluten-Free All-Purpose Baking Flour: This premixed flour combination is so superior to other mixes that we would collapse in a tear-drenched tantrum if they ever stopped making it. Love you, Bob!

Garbanzo–fava bean flour: A key player when combined with other starches to replicate the results of wheat flour. I generally prefer it to rice flour because it gives breads a great rise.

Brown rice flour: This starch is composed of finely ground unhulled rice kernels. It is gluten-free and typically yields a dense, grainy crumb.

Coconut flour: Coconut flour is gluten-free. It can be added to recipes to raise protein and fiber levels and to reduce overall carbohydrates. At BabyCakes NYC, it is an ingredient in the frosting because it is an excellent thickener that is unmatched in quality and taste.

Spelt flour: Spelt is wheat's distant cousin. Many people with delayed hypersensitivities to wheat, and even a number of people allergic to regular wheat, find spelt protein much easier to digest than wheat protein. Spelt, however, contains gluten, so it is *not* suitable for those on a gluten-free, wheat-free diet.

White spelt flour is made from spelt that has had the germ and bran removed. For recipes in which a lighter texture is wanted, like biscuits and strawberry shortcakes, I opt for white spelt flour; otherwise, I use whole spelt flour.

Potato starch: An ideal alternative to cornstarch, it thickens and adds moisture to baked goods.

Arrowroot: An excellent thickener that can be used in place of cornstarch to add smoothness. Great for its mild flavor and digestibility.

Baking powder: Not all baking powders are gluten-free, so be sure to check the label before you use a brand.

Kosher salt: You might not know it, but BabyCakes NYC is *certified* kosher, parve, and vegan!

Unsweetened cocoa powder: Not to be confused with regular cocoa mix, which contains sugar. Make sure to get a natural unsweetened cocoa powder that is not Dutch processed or alkalized, as those ingredients do not react with baking soda.

Xanthan gum: Used in tiny amounts, xanthan gum gives gluten-free batter viscosity and stickiness. Without it, your cakes and cookies will fall apart into sad crumbles. Simply, you must make your relationship with xanthan gum work at any cost.

Agave nectar: This natural sweetener is produced in Mexico from blue agave, salmiana, green, gray, thorny, or rainbow variety cactus. Agave nectar is much sweeter than honey and has a lovely fluid consistency. It's our favorite sweetener because it takes longer to absorb into the bloodstream, so it doesn't shoot your blood sugar up the way refined sugars do.

Evaporated cane juice: This is a sugar-based ingredient. There are times when agave doesn't provide the texture I'm looking for, and the evaporated crystals from cane juice are a prime substitute. Although it is derived from sugarcane, it isn't processed to the same degree as refined sugar and therefore retains more of the nutrients found in cane sugar.

Coconut oil: Our favored fat in the bakery, coconut oil is high in omega-3 fatty acids (these are healthy!), is packed with lauric acid, stores in your body as energy and not fat, and supports the proper function of the thyroid, thus stimulating the metabolism. It's a bit pricey, but so are the heart attacks it helps prevent.

Vanilla: Because many brands of vanilla are filtered with gluten-filled, grain-based alcohol, make sure to find a gluten-free brand you're comfortable with.

Vegan cheddar cheese: The best vegan cheeses melt well and maintain their flavor in the process.

Chocolate chips: My favorites are Ghirardelli semisweet chocolate chips.

Rice milk: A great vegan, soy-free alternative to milk.

Soy milk: If you are okay with soy, you can use it instead of rice milk, as it is a bit creamier.

Dry soy milk: Along with coconut flour, this is a primary ingredient in our world-famous frosting. It gives a thick and creamy quality many people prefer to real buttercream.

Coconut milk: Substituting coconut milk for rice or soy milk yields an incredibly rich product.

Apple cider vinegar: Made from pulverized apples, this is the only vinegar I use in my recipes. Mixed with rice milk, it is a great substitute for buttermilk.

Flax meal: Generally used to boost fiber and nutrition in recipes. I use it as a substitute for eggs in some muffins and cookies.

ADVICE ON INGREDIENT SUBSTITUTIONS

Of course, it is your prerogative to replace any of the ingredients in my recipes with others you are most comfortable using, but I can't guarantee the results. While testing recipes for this cookbook, I tried substitutes for some of the more costly ingredients, and the results were simply not up to par. That said, pennies are pennies, and you may find a bargain in some ingredient substitutions. Here are a few options that I found yielded results similar to the original.

- **Milk:** We primarily use rice milk, but coconut milk and soy milk can be used if your diet requires. Substitute the milk of your choice in equal measure, but be aware that any substitution will likely affect both the thickness and the sweetness of your batter. Adjust accordingly.

- **Sweeteners:** You can swap agave nectar for evaporated cane juice, and vice versa. One cup evaporated cane juice equals ¾ cup agave nectar. When replacing 1 cup evaporated cane juice with ¾ cup agave nectar, reduce the milk in the recipe by ¼ cup (oil measure remains the same). When using evaporated cane juice instead of agave nectar, add ¾ cup hot water to compensate for the lost moisture.

- **Oils:** If you are unable to use coconut oil, avocado, grapeseed, and pumpkin seed oil are all healthy choices, but canola oil is the most price-conscious option. You may also oil your pans with a nonstick spray. If you are gluten intolerant, be sure to use a plain formula and not one made for baking, as the latter contains wheat.

- **Flours:** Rice flour can be substituted in equal measure for garbanzo–fava bean flour. Neither spelt nor Bob's Red Mill Gluten-Free All-Purpose Flour, however, can stand in for garbanzo–fava bean flour.

MEASUREMENTS

Remember, baking is a science as much as it is an art, and precise measurements are crucial. You will save countless dollars and endless hours if you follow a few simple rules when making the recipes in this book.

All quantities in these recipes were measured in dry-ingredient measuring cups, including liquids. Never use clear measuring cups with a spout and a handle (in baking circles, known as *liquid measuring cups*). Trust me, the difference is real.

Always fill measuring cups evenly; do not approximate.

Always use proper measuring spoons. The teaspoons and tablespoons in your silverware drawer won't cut it, and eyeballed or otherwise rough measurements will result in baked goods so terrible and ugly I don't even want to discuss it.

SPELT VERSUS GLUTEN-FREE

If you have made your way into the bakery, or even just read press clippings or browsed our menu at www.babycakesnyc.com, you know we use either spelt flour or gluten-free flour in all our recipes. It's important to understand the difference between them before deciding which recipes are best suited to your needs.

Gluten is the protein found in grains such as wheat, barley, and rye. It provides structure, elasticity, and texture in breads. Unfortunately, it also provides millions of people with a variety of digestive and general health maladies.

Spelt is an ancient and distant ancestor to wheat, and it contains some of the same properties, including gluten. However, many people with wheat sensitivities are able to digest spelt comfortably and appreciate that it is high in complex carbohydrates, lower in overall carbohydrates, and contains enzymes that assist in glucose and insulin secretion. I am one of these people. This is why I use spelt flour in several of the recipes I've included in this book. I do not, however, encourage people who are wheat intolerant to consume spelt or spelt-based flour unless they've received the go-ahead from a doctor or a nutritionist.

Throughout this cookbook, only those recipes that call for the ingredient *spelt flour* contain gluten. At BabyCakes NYC, I go to great measures to ensure that there is no cross-contamination between the spelt flour and the rest of the bakery. We maintain separate mixing bowls, whisks, spatulas, measuring utensils, baking pans, sheet trays, sinks, and sponges all clearly labeled "Spelt" or "Gluten-Free."

Again, if you've been diagnosed with gluten allergies, it is important to consult your doctor before indulging in any of the spelt-based recipes in this cookbook. I've clearly indicated what type of flour is used in each recipe, so please, please read them closely. Agreed? Okay, then!

MUFI

Sweet
&
Savory $

CHAPTER NO. 1

muffins

○ ○

Considering my affinity for sweets, snacks, and everything in between, staying light on my toes hasn't always been easy. When I was nineteen, in a cruel manifestation of the "freshman 15," my once-miniature buns threatened to overtake the waistband of my favorite Frankie B jeans, emulating the beloved muffin tops that were the corner-stone of my high school diet. It took me a while to pinpoint the cause of this inflationary trend, as I believed muffins were a healthy alternative to bear claws and that a sugary mochaccino or three would pick up the tab for a lazy metabolism! Of course, now we all know that muffins are just handsomely packaged hunks of cake—not really the smartest way to start the day.

But a life without muffins was simply not an option for me. When I began creating recipes for BabyCakes NYC, devising muffin recipes that reached the same wondrous heights as those of my youth yet satisfied my new dietary restraints was at the top of the list. Right off the bat, swapping the traditional pound-packing ingredients for more health-conscious ones sent the calorie count plummeting; better still, the higher protein content of garbanzo–fava bean flour delivers nutrition that is absorbed into the bloodstream at a comparatively slower rate, preventing a spike in blood sugar and helping ward off the kind of midmorning hunger pangs brought on by your average *pain au chocolat*.

Best of all, these muffins are delicious by any standard. The tops are crisp, the insides billowy. They're everything you've hoped a muffin could be—and less.

○ ○

apple-
cinnamon muffins

To me, apple muffins that offer up a mouthful of mealy mashed apple chunks are a personal affront. Fortunately, such abominations are easily avoided, a simple matter of proper fruit selection. Forget for a minute your preferences when choosing an apple to eat out of hand (I'm talking to you, Red Delicious loyalists). For this recipe, you can't go wrong with tart, substantial Granny Smiths, especially when they've been roasted to caramelized perfection. If you prefer something sweeter, go halfsies with Granny Smith and either Pink Lady or Fuji, both of which deliver a fragrant bonus and add a depth of flavor even the ordinarily oblivious will notice.

○ **Makes 12** ○ ○ ○ ○ ○

Roasted Apples

1 POUND GRANNY SMITH APPLES, PEELED, CORED, AND DICED INTO 1-INCH CUBES

1 POUND PINK LADY APPLES, PEELED, CORED, AND DICED INTO 1-INCH CUBES

1 TABLESPOON GROUND CINNAMON

½ CUP AGAVE NECTAR

¼ CUP FRESH LEMON JUICE

Muffins

2 CUPS BOB'S RED MILL GLUTEN-FREE ALL-PURPOSE BAKING FLOUR

2 TEASPOONS BAKING POWDER

2 TEASPOONS BAKING SODA

1 TEASPOON XANTHAN GUM

1 TEASPOON SALT

2 TABLESPOONS GROUND CINNAMON

¼ TEASPOON GROUND NUTMEG

½ CUP COCONUT OIL

⅔ CUP AGAVE NECTAR

⅔ CUP RICE MILK

2 TABLESPOONS PURE VANILLA EXTRACT

Preheat the oven to 325°F. Line a baking sheet with parchment paper.

In a medium bowl, toss together the apples, cinnamon, agave nectar, and lemon juice until the apples are completely coated. Spread the mixture over the prepared baking sheet.

Bake the apples on the center rack for 35 minutes, rotating the sheet 180 degrees after 20 minutes. The apples will be soft. Let the apples stand for 30 minutes, or until completely cool. (The roasted apples can be stored in an airtight container in the refrigerator for up to 1 week.)

Keep the oven temperature at 325°F. Line a standard 12-cup muffin tin with paper liners.

In a medium bowl, whisk together the flour, baking powder, baking soda, xanthan gum, salt, cinnamon, and nutmeg. Add the oil, agave nectar, rice milk, and vanilla to the dry ingredients and stir until the batter is smooth. Add 1 cup of the roasted apples and stir to distribute.

Pour ⅓ cup batter into each prepared cup. Bake the muffins on the center rack for 22 minutes, rotating the tin 180 degrees after 15 minutes. The finished muffins will be golden brown, and a toothpick inserted in the center will come out clean.

Let the muffins stand in the tin for 15 minutes, then transfer them to a wire rack and cool completely. Store the muffins in an airtight container at room temperature for up to 3 days.

peach
corn muffins

synonymous with either the flabby pink shavings plopped beside a sushi roll or
a you were given on your sickbed. For years, I snubbed the root on those grounds,
but after opening the bakery, I quickly found I was in the minority. Here's the thing you need to
remember about baking with ginger: It needs a sidekick, or even two. For me, a subtle peach, baked
to sweet surrender, is the ideal complement to ginger's perfumy heat. For this recipe, corn bread is
the naturally sweet and grainy foundation.

o o o o o o o o o o o o o o o o o o o o o o o o o o o o o o o o o o o o o o o o o o o o o o   *Makes 12*   o o o o

Roasted Peaches

**4 CUPS SLICED FRESH PEACHES, WITH
SKIN REMAINING**

⅓ CUP AGAVE NECTAR

2 TABLESPOONS FRESH LEMON JUICE

Muffins

⅔ CUP RICE MILK

1 TABLESPOON APPLE CIDER VINEGAR

**1 CUP BOB'S RED MILL GLUTEN-FREE ALL-
PURPOSE BAKING FLOUR**

1 CUP CORNMEAL

2 TEASPOONS BAKING POWDER

2 TEASPOONS BAKING SODA

¾ TEASPOON XANTHAN GUM

1 TEASPOON SALT

1 TEASPOON GROUND CINNAMON

1 TABLESPOON GROUND GINGER

½ CUP COCONUT OIL

¾ CUP AGAVE NECTAR

**⅓ CUP HOMEMADE APPLESAUCE
(PAGE 78) OR STORE-BOUGHT
UNSWEETENED APPLESAUCE**

1 TABLESPOON PURE VANILLA EXTRACT

Preheat the oven to 325°F. Line a baking sheet with parchment
paper.

In a medium bowl, toss together the peaches, agave nectar,
and lemon juice. Spread the peaches evenly on the prepared
baking sheet and bake on the center rack for 20 minutes,
rotating the sheet 180 degrees after 12 minutes. The peaches
will be sizzling, with caramelized edges.

Let the peaches stand for 30 minutes, or until cool.

Keep the oven temperature at 325°F. Line a standard 12-cup
muffin tin with paper liners.

Pour the rice milk and apple cider vinegar into a small bowl.
Do not stir; set aside to develop into "buttermilk."

In a medium bowl, whisk together the flour, cornmeal, baking
powder, baking soda, xanthan gum, salt, cinnamon, and ginger. Add
the oil, agave nectar, applesauce, and vanilla to the dry ingredients and stir until the batter is smooth. Pour in the "buttermilk"
and mix gently just until the ingredients are fully incorporated.

Pour ⅓ cup batter into each prepared cup, almost filling it.
Top each muffin with 2 or 3 roasted peach wedges. Bake the
muffins on the center rack for 22 minutes, rotating the tin
180 degrees after 10 minutes. The finished muffins will be golden,
and a toothpick inserted in the center will come out clean.

Let the muffins stand in the tin for 15 minutes, then
transfer them to a wire rack and cool completely. Store the
muffins in an airtight container at room temperature for up to
3 days.

Working with **Fruits & Vegetables**

Although baking is a relatively precise science, there is some room for improvisation when it comes to the fruits and vegetables you add to your batters. If you choose to experiment with our formulas, observing the basic ratios of ingredient to batter below will spare you endless batches of trash can—bound batter.

Blueberries, raspberries, and cherries: Use fresh cherries when possible, but in a pinch go with a frozen organic variety. In many instances, I find frozen berries add significant volume without the marbled, juice—soaked effect they have when defrosted—or even fresh. Add $1/3$ cup berries per 1 cup flour.

Bananas: Unless you see actual mold on your bananas, they are fine to be used; they cannot be too ripe. Add 1 cup mashed (some chunks will remain) banana per 1 cup flour. For a denser bread, add an additional $1/3$ cup banana and reduce either the rice milk or the agave nectar by $1/4$ cup (I like to cut back on the agave nectar in these instances). If you prefer a lighter, fluffier product, reduce the banana to $2/3$ cup per 1 cup flour.

Carrots and zucchini: Grated carrots and zucchini both add a ton of moisture to recipes, and in doing so they extend the shelf life of muffins and teacakes tremendously. Use 1 cup grated, unpeeled vegetables per 1 cup flour. If you prefer a heartier bread, increase the carrot or zucchini by $1/4$ cup per 1 cup flour.

Apples, pears, and peaches: These add great caramelized texture when roasted in advance. To make your batter extra moist, mash half of the roasted fruit before adding it to the batter. It will give a hint of flavor along with lasting moistness (see "Making Applesauce and Other Purées," page 78). Add $1/2$ cup roasted fruit per 1 cup flour.

Rhubarb: This super—tangy vegetable is surprisingly delicious, but in my opinion it should be paired with fruit such as strawberries, raspberries, or apples to temper its sharp taste. Use 2 parts rhubarb to 1 part fruit for 2 cups flour.

pumpkin-spice muffins

When customers started requesting pumpkin-spice recipes, I turned to my brother Danny, the McKenna clan's resident Halloween expert and culinary school graduate. Danny's rule: The flavor of a pumpkin purée must be nutty and rich without being overly spicy or dense. Ever the pragmatist, and much to Danny's purist chagrin, I find that canned pumpkin purée is surprisingly flavorful and far more convincing than other canned vegetables. Sorry, Danny, but it's true.

Makes 12

2 CUPS BOB'S RED MILL GLUTEN-FREE ALL-PURPOSE BAKING FLOUR

2 TEASPOONS BAKING POWDER

2 TEASPOONS BAKING SODA

1 TEASPOON XANTHAN GUM

1 TEASPOON SALT

1 TABLESPOON GROUND CINNAMON

1 TABLESPOON GROUND GINGER

½ CUP COCONUT OIL, PLUS MORE FOR THE PAN

⅔ CUP AGAVE NECTAR

⅔ CUP RICE MILK

2 TABLESPOONS PURE VANILLA EXTRACT

1½ CUPS CANNED UNSWEETENED PUMPKIN PURÉE

½ CUP HOT WATER

Preheat the oven to 325°F. Line a standard 12-cup muffin tin with paper liners.

In a medium bowl, whisk together the flour, baking powder, baking soda, xanthan gum, salt, cinnamon, and ginger. Add the oil, agave nectar, rice milk, and vanilla to the dry ingredients. Stir until the batter is smooth and thick. Using a plastic spatula, fold in the pumpkin and hot water until both are evenly distributed throughout the batter.

Pour ⅓ cup batter into each prepared cup, almost filling it. Bake the muffins on the center rack for 22 minutes, rotating the tin 180 degrees after 10 minutes. The finished muffins will be soft to the touch, and a toothpick inserted in the center will come out clean.

Let the muffins stand in the tin for 15 minutes, then transfer them to a wire rack and cool completely. Store the muffins in an airtight container at room temperature for up to 3 days.

zucchini muffins

In my more rebellious stages, I wouldn't have touched a zucchini muffin with a 10-foot spiked-leather glove. But as Black Sabbath tendencies have given way to Doobie Brothers practices, this comforting spiced muffin has become a staple. By adjusting the amount of zucchini, you can alter the loaf's moisture. For a lighter bread, reduce the zucchini by 1/2 cup. (Before you do, though, keep in mind that this versatile vegetable is rich in potassium, which keeps muscles strong, regulates blood pressure, and mellows anxieties—it's something we could all do with a little more of.)

o o o o o o o o o o o o o o o o o o o o o o o o o o o o o o o o o o o **Makes 12** o o o o

2 CUPS WHOLE SPELT FLOUR

1/2 CUP FLAX MEAL

2 TEASPOONS BAKING POWDER

2 TEASPOONS BAKING SODA

1 TEASPOON SALT

2 TEASPOONS GROUND CINNAMON

1 TABLESPOON GROUND GINGER

1/2 CUP COCONUT OIL

3/4 CUP AGAVE NECTAR

3/4 CUP RICE MILK

1 TABLESPOON PURE VANILLA EXTRACT

2 CUPS SHREDDED ZUCCHINI

Preheat the oven to 325°F. Line a standard 12-cup muffin tin with paper liners.

In a medium bowl, whisk together the flour, flax meal, baking powder, baking soda, salt, cinnamon, and ginger. Add the oil, agave nectar, rice milk, and vanilla to the dry ingredients and stir until the batter is smooth. Using a plastic spatula, gently fold in the zucchini just until evenly distributed throughout the mixture.

Pour 1/3 cup batter into each prepared cup, almost filling it. Bake the muffins on the center rack for 22 minutes, rotating the tin 180 degrees after 15 minutes. The finished muffins will bounce back slightly when pressed, and a toothpick inserted in the center will come out clean.

Let the muffins stand in the tin for 15 minutes, then transfer them to a wire rack and cool completely. Store the muffins in an airtight container at room temperature for up to 3 days.

blueberry muffins

Is there anything better than having older sisters? When Kathy and Suzi left for college in Northern California, we younger sisters were shipped off for monthlong summer visits. With Kathy, days were spent ripping around in her Honda sedan, blasting Prince, popping doughnut holes by the bucketful, and making emergency stops at Contempo Casual. After we blew our babysitting money on stretch pants, we'd head over to Suzi's and rehab our sugar hangovers by getting back to nature. We'd raft down to the grocery store (seriously) and take leisurely bike rides. Suzi's pantry was stuffed with strange cereals (where were the neon-purple pieces?), whole-wheat pancake mix, and blueberry muffins. Bridget immediately went on a hunger strike, while I snuck snacks in the laundry room, discovering this new world of health-minded food. I quickly fell for the blueberry muffin, and it's been a close friend ever since. What follows is my version—it's light and sweet and I think you'll find it perfect for nearly every occasion.

o o o o o o o o o o o o o o o o o o o o o o o o o o o o o o o o o o o o o o o Makes 12 o o o o

2¼ CUPS WHOLE SPELT FLOUR
2 TEASPOONS BAKING POWDER
1 TEASPOON BAKING SODA
1 TEASPOON SALT
½ CUP COCONUT OIL
⅔ CUP AGAVE NECTAR
⅔ CUP RICE MILK
2 TEASPOONS PURE VANILLA EXTRACT
1 TEASPOON PURE LEMON EXTRACT
⅔ CUP FRESH BLUEBERRIES

Preheat the oven to 325°F. Line a standard 12-cup muffin tin with paper liners.

In a medium bowl, whisk together the flour, baking powder, baking soda, and salt. Add the oil, agave nectar, rice milk, vanilla, and lemon extract to the dry ingredients and stir until the batter is smooth. Using a plastic spatula, gently fold in the blueberries just until they are evenly distributed throughout the batter.

Pour ⅓ cup batter into each prepared cup, almost filling it. Bake the muffins on the center rack for 22 minutes, rotating the tin 180 degrees after 15 minutes. The finished muffins will bounce back slightly when pressed, and a toothpick inserted in the center will come out clean.

Let the muffins stand in the tin for 15 minutes, then transfer them to a wire rack and cool completely. Store the muffins in an airtight container at room temperature for up to 3 days.

CHAPTER NO. 2

biscuits & scones

o o o o o o o o o o o o o o o o o o o o o o o o o o o o o o o o o

nothing in the bakery garners more attention than straight-from-the-oven biscuits and scones. Savvy bakery-goers often look right past the display case and into the cooling rack, commandeering as many as we'll give them. Friends and family will have a similar response in your home.

Fledgling bakers assume that making biscuits and scones is a complicated and labor-intensive matter, and with good reason. Traditional recipes require a certain amount of coddling, with a lengthy procedure and equally lengthy baking time. In comparison, my recipes bake up quickly and are made with just four primary ingredients: spelt flour, baking powder, agave nectar, and coconut oil. If you've already stocked your pantry according to the list on pages 18–21, it's entirely possible for you to pull perfect biscuits or scones out of your oven 20 minutes from now!

Of course, my recipes are not exempt from the fundamental rules of biscuit and scone baking. Just as with conventional scones, overkneading will always make them tough. Adding too much or too little water will make them turn out shockingly flat or far too dense, respectively, so mind those measurements. Here's a good rule of thumb: As soon as you begin to wonder if your dough is fully incorporated, it is; give it a last tumble and move forward.

o o o o o o o o o o o o o o o o o o o o o o o o o o o o o o o o o

spelt Biscuits

By fifth grade, I'd taken to pocketing my lunch money and starving through the day so I could afford to spend the afternoons in the air-conditioned luxury of the local KFC and postpone the sweltering walk home. I'd buy a biscuit, fashion a "free" lemonade (1 cup ice water, 2 packets lemon juice, 27 or so sugar packets), swing my Capezios up onto the banquette of a comfy booth, and bask in my own genius. I don't know that the eventual walk was any better, but I do know I started a trend among other ponytailed rebels. With the biscuit bar set pretty high and KFC no longer an option or a preference, I assigned myself the challenge of bettering it with my allergy-friendly pantry. It's not uncommon these days for people to taste the biscuits at BabyCakes NYC and say, "These are better than KFC!"—and when they do, I execute a victory pirouette and shotgun a frosty glass of agave lemonade (page 133).

○ Makes 8 ○ ○ ○ ○

2 CUPS WHITE SPELT FLOUR, PLUS MORE FOR DUSTING

1 TABLESPOON BAKING POWDER

1 TEASPOON SALT, PLUS MORE FOR SPRINKLING

⅓ CUP COCONUT OIL, PLUS MORE FOR BRUSHING

¾ CUP HOT WATER

Preheat the oven to 375°F. Line a baking sheet with parchment paper.

In a medium bowl, whisk together the flour, baking powder, and salt. Pour the oil and hot water into the dry ingredients and mix with a rubber spatula until fully combined and a dough is formed. If the batter is dry, add more hot water, 2 tablespoons at a time, until the dough is sticky.

Dust the counter with spelt flour. Place the dough on the prepared surface and drag it through the flour. Pat the dough gently until it is 1 inch thick. Using a 3-inch round cookie cutter, cut out biscuits and arrange them on the prepared baking sheet, leaving 1 inch between the biscuits so they can spread. Brush each with oil and sprinkle with salt. Bake the biscuits on the center rack for 8 minutes, rotating the sheet 180 degrees after 4 minutes. The finished biscuits will have a golden, flaky crust.

Let the biscuits stand on the sheet for 5 minutes before serving. Cool completely and store in plastic wrap at room temperature for up to 2 days.

Advanced **Biscuitry**

The basic biscuit recipe is just the beginning of a long and rewarding friendship. Try running through the process a few times—and then get creative! To help you begin, here are a few of my favorite variations.

Savory

- On Thanksgiving, I infuse my biscuit batter with a handful of chopped sage and fresh cracked pepper, which pairs perfectly with nearly every dish you'll find at a holiday table. Other herbs that work equally well are chives, marjoram, and rosemary.

- Another option is to brush the biscuits with coconut oil and top with grated vegan cheese before baking. These are great fresh out of the oven, and the cheese helps seal in the moisture to keep them delicious for days.

- Fold in ½ cup grated zucchini to raise the nutritional level and add moisture. Although the biscuits will be slightly more dense, the surprising flavor and texture more than compensate.

Sweet

- There's nothing I love more than the pairing of salty and sweet. On special occasions, before we put the biscuits in the oven, we sprinkle a few with cinnamon and evaporated cane juice, and they come out tasting better than doughnuts.

- Try dredging the biscuits in cornmeal before placing them on your baking sheet. Brush with oil and salt and proceed with the baking instructions. Once they are done, brush with agave nectar to finish.

- If you're looking to add fruit to your breakfast, fold blueberries or apples into your biscuit dough and sprinkle with the spice of your choice.

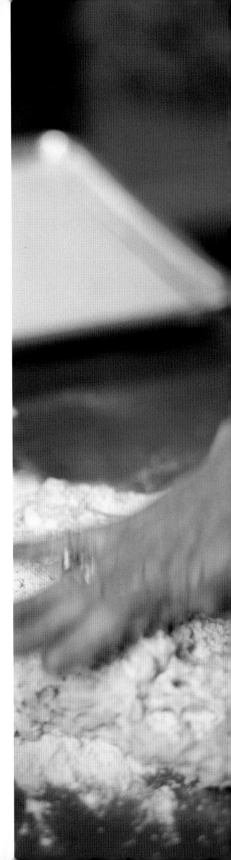

strawberry shortcake

Whoever is responsible for the trend of subbing store-bought miniature angel-food cakes for shortcake in strawberry shortcake should be called in for questioning. Angel food's rubbery texture does nothing for the berry, and once it has absorbed any moisture at all, it becomes a soggy sponge that leaves you reaching for a toothbrush rather than seconds. BabyCakes NYC's rich, flaky shortcake is a perfect showcase for luscious strawberries. If the vanilla frosting is too sweet for you in the morning, the lighter vanilla sauce (page 91) can be used with equal success. Did global warming ruin your summer fruit crop? Go with your favorite fruit preserves instead.

o o o o o o o o o o o o o o o o o o o o o o o o o o o o o o o o o o o o o   *Makes 12*   o o o o

3 CUPS WHITE SPELT FLOUR,
PLUS ½ CUP FOR DUSTING

½ CUP EVAPORATED CANE JUICE

1½ TABLESPOONS BAKING POWDER

1 TEASPOON SALT

7 TABLESPOONS COCONUT OIL

1 TABLESPOON PURE VANILLA EXTRACT

⅔ CUP HOT WATER

VANILLA FROSTING (PAGE 91)

1½ CUPS STEMMED AND SLICED
FRESH STRAWBERRIES

Preheat the oven to 350°F. Line 2 baking sheets with parchment paper.

In a medium bowl, whisk together the flour, evaporated cane juice, baking powder, and salt. Add the oil, vanilla, and hot water to the dry ingredients. Combine until a slightly moist dough is formed.

Dust the counter generously with spelt flour. Roll the dough through the flour until it is coated on all sides. Gently pat the dough into a 1-inch-thick rectangle and cut out 12 shortcakes with a 3-inch round cookie cutter. Place the shortcakes about 1 inch apart on the prepared baking sheets. Bake the shortcakes on the center rack for 16 minutes, rotating the sheets 180 degrees after 9 minutes. The finished shortcakes will have a slightly golden, flaky crust.

Let the shortcakes cool on the sheets for 15 minutes, or until completely cool. Cut them in half horizontally and spread each side with 1 tablespoon vanilla frosting using a small offset spatula. Spoon 1 generous tablespoon strawberries onto one of the halves and top with the second half. Garnish with more frosting and strawberries. Store the filled shortcakes in an airtight container at room temperature for up to 2 days.

raspberry
scones

This is as close to a traditional scone as BabyCakes NYC comes. I 86'ed the butter, obviously, and played up the sweet, all without abandoning the light-yet-satisfying texture. I find that raspberries, more delicate than currants or other popular berries used in scones, have a tanginess that's a perfect accompaniment to morning tea.

o o o o o o o o o o o o o o o o o o o o o o o o o o o o o o o o o o *Makes 8* o o o o

2 CUPS WHOLE SPELT FLOUR

1 TABLESPOON BAKING POWDER

½ TEASPOON SALT

**⅓ CUP COCONUT OIL,
PLUS MORE FOR BRUSHING**

**⅓ CUP AGAVE NECTAR,
PLUS MORE FOR BRUSHING**

1 TABLESPOON PURE VANILLA EXTRACT

¼ CUP HOT WATER

1 CUP FRESH RASPBERRIES

Preheat the oven to 350°F. Line a baking sheet with parchment paper.

In a medium bowl, whisk together the flour, baking powder, and salt. Add the oil, agave nectar, and vanilla and stir together until a thick, slightly dry batter is formed. Pour the hot water into the batter and mix. Using a rubber spatula, gently fold in the raspberries just until they are marbled throughout the batter.

For each scone, scoop ⅓ cup batter onto the prepared baking sheet. Space the scoops 1 inch apart to allow them to spread. Lightly brush the tops with the oil. Bake the scones on the center rack for 14 minutes, rotating the sheet 180 degrees after 7 minutes. The finished scones will be golden and slightly firm. Remove from the oven and brush with agave nectar.

Let the scones stand on the sheet for 15 minutes, then carefully slide a spatula under each and transfer it to a wire rack and cool completely. Store the scones in an airtight container at room temperature for up to 2 days.

chocolate shortbread scones
with caramelized bananas

There are only five circumstances under which a person wants chocolate for breakfast:

1. You dumped your boyfriend or husband in a champagne-soaked tantrum the night before.

2. Based on the contents of your fridge, it's either chocolate sauce or a spoonful of mustard.

3. You are under the age of eight.

4. You are pregnant.

5. You have just whipped up a batch of these babies.

These scones are light and elegant compared to traditional scones, whose texture often sets my stomach on spin cycle.

Makes 12

Caramelized Bananas

6 MEDIUM BANANAS, THINLY SLICED LENGTHWISE AND CUT IN HALF

¼ CUP AGAVE NECTAR

½ TEASPOON GROUND CINNAMON

½ TEASPOON SALT

Chocolate Shortbread Scones

1 CUP CHOCOLATE CRUMB BASE (PAGE 116)

¼ CUP VEGAN CHOCOLATE CHIPS

2½ CUPS WHOLE SPELT FLOUR, PLUS MORE FOR DUSTING

½ CUP UNSWEETENED COCOA POWDER

½ CUP EVAPORATED CANE JUICE, PLUS MORE FOR SPRINKLING

1½ TABLESPOONS BAKING POWDER

1 TEASPOON SALT

½ CUP COCONUT OIL, PLUS ¼ CUP FOR BRUSHING

1 TABLESPOON PURE VANILLA EXTRACT

⅓ CUP HOT WATER

VANILLA FROSTING (PAGE 91)

½ CUP VEGAN CONFECTIONERS' SUGAR

Preheat the oven to 350°F. Line a baking sheet with parchment paper.

In a medium bowl, gently mix together the bananas, agave nectar, cinnamon, and salt until the bananas are completely coated.

Spread the banana mixture over the prepared baking sheet. Bake the bananas on the center rack for 20 minutes. The edges of the banana slices will be crisp and golden brown. Remove from the oven. Let the bananas stand for 30 minutes, or until completely cool. (The bananas can be stored in an airtight container in the refrigerator for up to 1 week.)

Line 2 baking sheets with parchment paper.

In a small bowl, mix together the chocolate crumb and chocolate chips just until combined; set aside. In a medium bowl, whisk together the flour, cocoa powder, evaporated cane juice, baking powder, and salt. Add ½ cup oil, the vanilla, and the hot water and combine until a thick dough is formed. If the mixture seems too dry, fold additional water, 1 tablespoon at a time, into the batter until it is moist. Using a plastic spatula, gently fold the chocolate chip–crumb mix into the dough just until it appears marbled.

(continues)

Dust the counter generously with flour. Drag the dough through the flour until it is completely coated. Pat the dough gently until it is 1 inch thick, and, using a 3-inch round cookie cutter, make 12 scones. Arrange the scones on the prepared baking sheets with at least 1 inch between them. Brush each with the remaining ¼ cup oil and sprinkle them with a pinch of evaporated cane juice. Bake the scones on the center rack for 18 minutes, rotating the sheets 180 degrees after 10 minutes. The finished scones will be crisp to the touch.

Let the scones cool on the sheets for 30 minutes, or until completely cool. Cut each scone in half horizontally and spread 1 tablespoon vanilla frosting and a generous amount of the caramelized bananas on the bottom half. Replace the tops and dust with confectioners' sugar. Store the scones in an airtight container at room temperature for up to 2 days.

LOVE FROM THE FAN CLUB:
Natalie Portman

It is my distinct honor to present to you an enchanting and gifted actress, a committed activist, a renowned cruelty-free cobbler (have you seen her leather-free line of shoes, Beyond Skin?! So great!): Oh, you know it's Natalie Portman, don't even kid!

When I became a vegan, I thought I'd never eat anything sweet and tasty outside of fruit and sorbet again. I'd become resigned to the sweetness of nature's low-hanging fruit . . . until I was introduced to Baby-Cakes NYC. Suddenly, I was having delicious vegan hamantaschen on Purim. And miniature brownies that melted in my mouth. And these miraculous chocolate scones filled with frosting and caramelized bananas! It all tasted better than anything made with butter, cream, and eggs, and, equally important, it allowed me to indulge with a clear conscience. At BabyCakes NYC I can eat what I crave without harming my lovely animal friends—or myself. Ever since that first fateful day, I've been waiting for this cookbook. Now your secrets are mine, BabyCakes!

johnnycakes

If you are unfamiliar with johnnycakes, thank me now: Your life is about to change
others, pat yourselves on the back and grab a cookie sheet.) Part corn-bread panca
this New England breakfast staple stepped in to fill the void left when my pancake
short by gluten sensitivities. I drown mine in agave nectar, but no matter how you treat them, plan
on sharing. You only rarely find these at BabyCakes NYC because they absolutely must be served
warm. Although I bake them on a cookie sheet, you can spoon them onto a well-greased griddle for a
crisper—though more caloric—cake.

o o o o o o o o o o o o o o o o o o o o o o o o o o o o o o o o o o o o   *Makes 8*   o o o o

1½ CUPS WHOLE SPELT FLOUR

½ CUP CORNMEAL,
PLUS MORE FOR DUSTING

1 TABLESPOON BAKING POWDER

1 TEASPOON SALT, PLUS MORE
FOR SPRINKLING

⅓ CUP COCONUT OIL

2 TABLESPOONS AGAVE NECTAR,
PLUS MORE FOR DRIZZLING

1 TEASPOON PURE VANILLA EXTRACT

¼ CUP HOT WATER

Preheat the oven to 350°F. Line a baking sheet with parchment
paper.

In a medium bowl, whisk together the flour, cornmeal,
baking powder, and salt. Add the oil, 2 tablespoons agave nectar,
and vanilla to the dry ingredients and stir until the batter is
smooth. Pour the hot water over the mixture, and blend to make
a thick, grainy batter.

For each johnnycake, scoop ⅓ cup batter onto the prepared
baking sheet, spaced 1 inch apart. Sprinkle each with a pinch of
salt. Bake the johnnycakes on the center rack for 14 minutes,
rotating the sheet 180 degrees after 7 minutes. The edges of the
finished johnnycakes will be golden brown and firm to the touch.

Let the johnnycakes stand on the sheet for 10 minutes, then
drizzle with agave nectar. Transfer to a wire rack and cool
completely. Store the cooled johnnycakes in an airtight container,
separated by layers of parchment paper, at room temperature
for up to 2 days.

CHAPTER NO. 3

teacakes

○ ○

I magine you and I are in many ways similar, and that, like me, in addition to being fairly awesome, you usually keep a snack of some kind stashed in your purse, at your desk, maybe even disintegrating into a pile of crumbs in your pocket. It's nothing to be ashamed of! What *is* a crying shame, though, is the sad state of the snack industry. Why be at the mercy of the vending machine down the hall? A slice of one of the light but satisfying teacakes in this chapter is what I grab on the way out the door, and I think it's safe to say that once you've made a few yourself, you'll be doing the same.

Adding teacakes to your repertoire may just serve you better than any other lesson you take away from this book. These recipes are mostly one-bowl affairs, and beyond their relative simplicity, what makes them so great is their humble, everyman quality. New to the baking game? These recipes are invaluable confidence-builders and a good way to get acquainted with fundamental techniques, measurements, and ingredients. As for you well-seasoned bakers, well, get ready for a total kitchen reprogramming, with recipes for a few loaves you can actually commit to memory and whip up at will.

I often bring a teacake or two along as gifts when I visit friends, though it's not an entirely selfless act; that way I'm guaranteed to have a quick bite on hand when I need one. A little high-maintenance? Probably, but some find it charming, too! (I do share, after all.) Try a few of these and join the club.

○ ○

corn bread

Some recipes at the bakery were brought forth by inspiration, others by customer demand. The lobbying for corn bread began the very first day of business, with a customer spying an unfrosted vanilla cupcake and ordering "one of those corn muffins." Rather than fight the will of the people, I dived right into development mode, and after a year of sorry results, finally perfected the recipe. I hope you'll agree it was well worth the effort.

o o o o o o o o o o o o o o o o o o o o o o o o o o o o o o o o o o o o *Makes 10 slices* o o o o

⅔ CUP RICE MILK

1 TABLESPOON APPLE CIDER VINEGAR

¾ CUP BOB'S RED MILL GLUTEN-FREE ALL-PURPOSE BAKING FLOUR

½ CUP CORNMEAL

½ CUP CORN FLOUR

2 TEASPOONS BAKING POWDER

1 TEASPOON BAKING SODA

1 TEASPOON XANTHAN GUM

1 TEASPOON SALT

½ CUP COCONUT OIL, PLUS MORE FOR THE PAN

⅓ CUP AGAVE NECTAR

⅓ CUP HOMEMADE APPLESAUCE (PAGE 78) OR STORE-BOUGHT UNSWEETENED APPLESAUCE

2 TEASPOONS PURE VANILLA EXTRACT

Preheat the oven to 325°F. Lightly grease a 7 x 4 x 3-inch loaf pan with oil.

Pour the rice milk and apple cider vinegar into a small bowl, but do not stir; set aside to develop into "buttermilk." In a medium bowl, whisk together the flour, cornmeal, corn flour, baking powder, baking soda, xanthan gum, and salt. Add the oil, agave nectar, applesauce, and vanilla to the dry ingredients. Stir the batter until well combined. Pour in the "buttermilk." Mix gently until the ingredients are fully incorporated and a slightly grainy batter is formed.

Pour the batter into the prepared pan. Bake the corn bread on the center rack for 32 minutes, rotating the pan 180 degrees after 20 minutes. The finished corn bread will bounce back slightly when pressed, and a toothpick inserted in the center will come out clean.

Let the corn bread stand in the pan for 20 minutes, then gently run a knife around the edge of the bread. Cover the top of the pan with a cutting board, and invert the loaf onto the board. Carefully lift the pan away and re-invert the corn bread onto another cutting board. Either cut and serve warm, or wait until completely cool before storing. Cover the uncut corn bread with plastic wrap and store at room temperature for up to 3 days.

Introducing Elizabeth McKenna,
my youngest sibling and
BabyCakes NYC's resident drama
untangler, PR genius,
and sweetie pie.

What started off as my daily wake-up
slice of corn bread is now a full-blown
obsession that borders on addiction.
Understand, I work in the bakery five
days a week, but on those other two days
I still manage to slip in, scan the counter,
and devour any available samples left out
for customers. When I pass the empty
plate sheepishly toward the counter
person and squish my face as if to say,
"I'm sorry," it's all a ruse. What I'm
really thinking is "More corn bread pieces,
please!" Later, when I unwrap a salty-
sweet morsel, friends look on with envy
and hope. It crosses my mind to offer
them some, but I usually don't. After all,
it's a very real possibility there won't be
any left when I make my final pass by the
bakery before bedtime.

jalapeño-cheddar corn bread

Embellishing a recipe as iconic as corn bread could be a disaster of New Coke magnitude, so when a friend suggested dolling up the recipe with jalapeños and cheddar cheese, I proceeded with caution. I have issues with vegan cheese—it's often overprocessed, packed with preservatives, and usually gross—but Emily, my office Queen Bee and resident persnickety vegan, suggested Follow Your Heart's cheddar and made me a convert. I found nary a gluten globule or preservative in sight, and it melted! My mind adequately blown, I got to work in the kitchen, and a new bakery regular emerged. The cheese has the perfect creamy texture to complement the corn bread's slightly grainy quality, and its sweetness is offset by the heat of the jalapeños. Bring this along to your next barbecue, but be sure to make extra: Those non-vegan eat-everything sorts tend to devour an unfair share.

Makes 10 slices

⅔ CUP RICE MILK

1 TABLESPOON APPLE CIDER VINEGAR

¾ CUP BOB'S RED MILL GLUTEN-FREE ALL-PURPOSE BAKING FLOUR

¾ CUP CORNMEAL

¼ CUP CORN FLOUR

2 TABLESPOONS BAKING POWDER

1 TEASPOON BAKING SODA

1 TEASPOON XANTHAN GUM

1 TEASPOON SALT

½ CUP COCONUT OIL, PLUS MORE FOR THE PAN

½ CUP AGAVE NECTAR

⅓ CUP HOMEMADE APPLESAUCE (PAGE 78) OR STORE-BOUGHT UNSWEETENED APPLESAUCE

1 TABLESPOON PURE VANILLA EXTRACT

¼ CUP SEEDED AND DICED JALAPEÑOS

⅔ CUP DICED VEGAN CHEDDAR CHEESE, ¼-INCH CUBES

Preheat the oven to 325°F. Lightly grease a 7 x 4 x 3-inch loaf pan with oil.

Pour the rice milk and apple cider vinegar into a small bowl, but do not stir; set aside to develop into "buttermilk." In a medium bowl, whisk together the flour, cornmeal, corn flour, baking powder, baking soda, xanthan gum, and salt. Add the oil, agave nectar, applesauce, and vanilla to the dry ingredients. Stir the batter until fully combined. Pour in the "buttermilk" and mix gently until the ingredients are fully incorporated and a slightly grainy batter is formed. Using a plastic spatula, fold in the jalapeños and cheese until evenly distributed throughout the batter.

Pour the batter into the prepared pan and bake the corn bread on the center rack for 40 minutes, rotating the pan 180 degrees after 20 minutes. The finished corn bread will bounce back slightly when pressed, and a toothpick inserted in the center will come out clean.

Let the corn bread stand in the pan for 20 minutes, then gently run a knife around the edge of the bread. Cover the top of the pan with a cutting board, and invert the loaf onto the board. Carefully lift the pan away and re-invert the corn bread onto another cutting board. Either cut and serve warm, or wait until it is completely cool before storing. Cover the uncut corn bread with plastic wrap and store at room temperature for up to 3 days.

Mary-Louise Parker

Bakers, I am pleased to present to you one of BabyCakes NYC's favorite regulars . . . MLP!

The BabyCakes NYC banana bread is the best I've ever had and something I simply can't live without. The fact that it's good for you is just a plus. It's one of those things you're eager to introduce to friends so they can herald you as some in-the-know genius. When I first brought a loaf on set, I told everyone it was vegan, and people shied away. After a bit of pressuring, they dug in, and I was suddenly fighting them off to get a piece for myself. This banana bread is an almost impossibly delicious godsend for vegans and children with food allergies alike.

banana bread /
banana chocolate chip bread

When my aunt Cathy dropped by our house for a visit and tea, she was always packing a loaf of banana bread baked at her restaurant, Harry's Coffee Shop, in La Jolla, California. Under her strong encouragement, I'd chow piece after piece until I'd scarfed nearly an entire loaf. "It's good for her!" she'd say as my mother looked on in slight horror. And I believed her. I mean, banana bread? Come on! Eating that pillowy deliciousness was like getting extra-credit points for free. Of course, in adulthood I discovered that this supposed health bread, like everything else tasty, was virtually a heart attack in loaf form. Butter? Eggs? Bleached flour? Sugar?! Aunt Cathy, take note: Below is how you do it while sparing yourself—and your behind—the grief. If you'd like to take this recipe to the next level, include 1 cup of chocolate chips when you add the banana. You will not be sorry.

o o o o o o o o o o o o o o o o o o o o o o o o o o o o o o o o   *Makes 10 slices*   o o o o

2 CUPS BOB'S RED MILL GLUTEN-FREE
ALL-PURPOSE BAKING FLOUR

2 TEASPOONS BAKING POWDER

2 TEASPOONS BAKING SODA

1 TEASPOON XANTHAN GUM

1 TEASPOON SALT

1 TEASPOON GROUND CINNAMON

½ CUP COCONUT OIL,
PLUS MORE FOR THE PAN

⅔ CUP AGAVE NECTAR

⅔ CUP RICE MILK

1 TEASPOON PURE VANILLA EXTRACT

6 MEDIUM BANANAS,
PEELED AND MASHED

Preheat the oven to 325°F. Lightly grease a 7 x 4 x 3-inch loaf pan with oil.

In a medium bowl, whisk together the flour, baking powder, baking soda, xanthan gum, salt, and cinnamon. Add ½ cup oil and the agave nectar, rice milk, and vanilla to the dry ingredients. Stir until the batter is smooth. Using a plastic spatula, gently fold in the bananas until they are evenly distributed throughout the batter.

Pour the batter into the prepared pan. Bake the banana bread on the center rack for 35 minutes, rotating the pan 180 degrees after 20 minutes. The finished loaf will bounce back slightly when pressed, and a toothpick inserted in the center will come out clean.

Let the banana bread stand in the pan for 20 minutes. Gently run a knife around the edge of the cake, cover the top of the pan with a cutting board, and invert the loaf onto the board. Carefully lift the pan away and re-invert the bread onto another cutting board. Either cut and serve warm, or wait until completely cool before storing. Cover the uncut banana bread with plastic wrap and store at room temperature for up to 3 days.

apple-cinnamon toastie

Until the bagel made its way across the San Diego County border from the East Coast and nudged its way into our bread box in the early 1980s, my mother's breakfast staple was a toasted slice of cinnamon-swirl bread, which she nibbled while sipping her morning coffee and skimming Dave Barry's latest effort. It was the only personal time we allowed her, however begrudgingly, and the scene is indelibly etched in my mind. In tribute to Mom, I came up with the apple-cinnamon toastie, now and forever a must-have on the bakery menu. Because it has a great crumb and is not too sweet, it's perfect for toasting and slathering with your favorite spread. Martha Stewart (yes, that one) liked it so much she asked me to teach her to make it. On her show!

○ Makes 10 slices ○ ○ ○ ○

1 CUP GARBANZO–FAVA BEAN FLOUR

1¼ CUPS EVAPORATED CANE JUICE, PLUS MORE FOR SPRINKLING

½ CUP POTATO STARCH

¼ CUP ARROWROOT

2¼ TEASPOONS BAKING POWDER

¼ TEASPOON BAKING SODA

½ TEASPOON XANTHAN GUM

1 TEASPOON SALT

2 TABLESPOONS GROUND CINNAMON

½ CUP COCONUT OIL, PLUS MORE FOR THE PAN AND FOR BRUSHING

⅓ CUP HOMEMADE APPLESAUCE (PAGE 78) OR STORE-BOUGHT UNSWEETENED APPLESAUCE

2 TABLESPOONS PURE VANILLA EXTRACT

1¼ CUPS HOT WATER

1 CUP ROASTED APPLES (PAGE 27)

Preheat the oven to 325°F. Lightly grease a 7 x 4 x 3-inch loaf pan with oil.

In a medium bowl, whisk together the flour, 1 cup of the evaporated cane juice, and the potato starch, arrowroot, baking powder, baking soda, xanthan gum, salt, and 1 tablespoon of the cinnamon. Add the oil, applesauce, vanilla, and 1 cup of the hot water to the dry ingredients. Stir until the batter is smooth, then fold in the roasted apples. Transfer ¼ cup of the batter to a small bowl, and add the remaining ¼ cup evaporated cane juice, 1 tablespoon cinnamon, and ¼ cup hot water. Stir until creamy.

Pour the apple batter into the prepared loaf pan. Carefully drizzle the batter from the small bowl down the center of the loaf. Use a teaspoon to swirl the topping into the loaf, moving the spoon up and down. Sprinkle the top with evaporated cane juice. Bake the toastie on the center rack for 25 minutes, remove from the oven, and brush the top with a generous amount of oil. Return to the oven and bake for another 15 minutes, until crunchy and a toothpick inserted in the center comes out clean.

Let the toastie stand in the pan for 20 minutes, then invert the cake onto a board. Turn right side up and cut and serve warm. Cover the cooled uncut toastie with plastic wrap and store at room temperature for up to 3 days.

lemon-poppy teacake

Lemon can be a baker's best friend or her worst enemy. Often it tastes less like fresh-squeezed lemonade and more like a 15-cent lollipop. Achieving the perfect balance of lemon flavor in this teacake was a long and arduous journey; fresh lemon juice toys with the acidity in the batter, causing it to rise and fall unpredictably, while the rind on its own has a mousy presence at best. I tried everything from the yellow squeeze bottles of sugar-pumped citric acid to preserved lemons to lemon oil—everything short of boiled-down Lemonheads. Eventually I found that if you grate lemon rind into the batter with a generous helping of a high-quality lemon extract (I prefer Frontier's product), you end up with a uniform, easy-to-manage batter that maximizes the lemon flavor while downplaying its domineering nature. Add the subtle nuttiness and earthy texture of poppy seeds, and you've stumbled onto a marriage unequaled since Luke and Laura's.

○ **Makes 10 slices** ○ ○ ○

⅔ CUP RICE MILK

1 TABLESPOON APPLE CIDER VINEGAR

¼ CUP POPPY SEEDS

¾ CUP BOB'S RED MILL GLUTEN-FREE ALL-PURPOSE BAKING FLOUR

½ CUP BROWN RICE FLOUR

1½ TABLESPOONS BAKING POWDER

1 TEASPOON XANTHAN GUM

1 TEASPOON SALT

½ CUP COCONUT OIL, PLUS MORE FOR THE PAN

¾ CUP AGAVE NECTAR

⅓ CUP HOMEMADE APPLESAUCE (PAGE 78) OR STORE-BOUGHT UNSWEETENED APPLESAUCE

1 TEASPOON PURE VANILLA EXTRACT

2 TABLESPOONS PURE LEMON EXTRACT

1 TABLESPOON GRATED LEMON ZEST

Preheat the oven to 325°F. Lightly grease a 7 x 4 x 3-inch loaf pan with oil.

Pour the rice milk, vinegar, and poppy seeds into a small bowl, but do not stir; set aside. In a medium bowl, whisk together the flours, baking powder, xanthan gum, and salt. Add the oil, agave nectar, applesauce, vanilla, lemon extract, and lemon zest to the dry ingredients and stir until the batter is smooth. Using a rubber spatula, scrape the poppy seed mixture into the batter, and combine just until all the ingredients are blended. The batter will expand slightly.

Pour the batter into the prepared pan and bake the teacake on the center rack for 35 minutes, rotating the pan 180 degrees after 18 minutes. The finished teacake will be golden brown and springy, and a toothpick inserted in the center will come out clean.

Let the teacake stand in the pan for 20 minutes, then gently run a knife around the edge of the cake. Cover the top of the pan with a cutting board, and invert the loaf onto the board. Carefully lift the pan away and re-invert the teacake onto another cutting board. Either cut and serve warm, or wait until it is completely cool before storing. Cover the uncut teacake with plastic wrap and store at room temperature for up to 3 days.

gingerbread

Those of you who don't have food sensitivities and are reading this cookbook simply to improve your general health should be applauded. I know how easy it is to be tricked into thinking that the low-fat glazed gingerbread in the display is healthy when you pick up your morning coffee at the local deli. I implore you, do not let your pre-caffeine fog steer you wrong! Make a loaf of this simple gingerbread over the weekend, slice it, and store it in your freezer for the week so you can grab yourself a piece on your way out the door. The pumpkin purée makes the bread so moist and fresh you can snack on it for days. As a reward for your foresight, consider slathering a thick layer of Vanilla Frosting (page 91) on top. I would!

○ *Makes 10 slices* ○ ○ ○

2 CUPS BOB'S RED MILL GLUTEN-FREE
ALL-PURPOSE BAKING FLOUR

2 TEASPOONS BAKING POWDER

2 TEASPOONS BAKING SODA

1 TEASPOON XANTHAN GUM

1 TEASPOON SALT

1 TEASPOON GROUND CINNAMON

2 TABLESPOONS GROUND GINGER

¼ TEASPOON GROUND NUTMEG

½ CUP COCONUT OIL,
PLUS MORE FOR THE PAN

⅔ CUP AGAVE NECTAR

¼ CUP MOLASSES

⅔ CUP RICE MILK

1 TABLESPOON PURE VANILLA EXTRACT

1⅓ CUPS CANNED UNSWEETENED
PUMPKIN PURÉE

¾ CUP HOT WATER

VANILLA FROSTING (PAGE 91)

Preheat the oven to 325°F. Lightly grease a 7 x 4 x 3-inch loaf pan with oil.

In a medium bowl, whisk together the flour, baking powder, baking soda, xanthan gum, salt, cinnamon, ginger, and nutmeg. Add the oil, agave nectar, molasses, rice milk, and vanilla to the dry ingredients and stir until the thick batter is smooth. Using a plastic spatula, gently fold in the pumpkin purée and hot water just until the batter is smooth.

Pour the batter into the prepared pan. Bake the gingerbread on the center rack for 40 minutes, rotating the pan 180 degrees after 20 minutes. The finished gingerbread will bounce back slightly when pressed, and a toothpick inserted in the center will come out clean.

Let the gingerbread stand in the pan for 20 minutes, then gently run a knife around the edge of the cake. Cover the top of the pan with a cutting board, and invert the loaf onto the board. Carefully lift the pan away, re-invert the gingerbread onto a wire rack, and cool completely. Using a frosting spatula, spread a thick layer of vanilla frosting over the top. Store the gingerbread in an airtight container in the refrigerator for up to 4 days.

Batter **Spectacular**

So you've got only a mini-loaf pan handy, or maybe you're looking to indulge a creative tick or dazzle a hungry guest. Here are a few ways to trick out your teacake batter:

Lemon poppy: Oil a mini-muffin tin and fill the cups two-thirds full with batter. Swirl in your favorite jam (blackberry and blueberry work best) and vegan cream cheese. The crunchy texture and creamy, sweet, tart center make a cute snack to pack in your child's lunch box—or to stash in your own desk drawer at work.

Banana bread: Line a cookie sheet with parchment paper and spread batter on it in a thin layer. Bake until it's cooked through, about 10 minutes. Let the cake cool before cutting it into sandwich-size squares. Slap your favorite spread—pumpkin seed butter and Chocolate Sauce (page 93) is my favorite combination—between two slices and go wild.

Gingerbread: Toss in 1 cup shredded carrot and ¼ cup flax meal to make it a covertly nutritional snack.

cookies
& brownies

○ ○

by now you know I'm an unabashed snacker, right? Large meals don't especially appeal to me, but only because it means I won't be hungry when the next opportunity to snack rolls around. Cookies and brownies are two of my absolute favorite ways to indulge this habit.

At the risk of sounding like a biased parent, I have to say that nothing in the bakery makes me happier or more proud than my cookie recipes. For all their simplicity and all the headaches they caused in the trial stages, I think they go far beyond even what I thought possible.

People often assume commercially produced vegan cookies are nutritious alternatives to Chips Ahoy, but this is not exactly the case. Despite clever marketing, most are relatively high in both fat and sugar, without having the common sense or the courtesy to taste that way. While our cookies and brownies can't claim to be health food, they do have numerous virtues that set them apart from the pack. I use flax meal to up the cookie's omega-3s, garbanzo—fava bean flour for added protein, and coconut oil to help regulate the metabolism—all while keeping fat to a minimum. Coconut oil mimics the flavor of butter almost perfectly, and you'd be hard-pressed to tell the difference between my version and your grandmother's when the tray comes out of the oven.

Brownies, too, are often given awkward treatment in health-conscious kitchens. Made without eggs, many recipes fail to compensate properly for the missing moisture and consequently produce dense, dry bites with a one-day shelf life. Applesauce is a simple, inexpensive answer to all these moisture and binding issues, but as added insurance, I tend to up the amount of chocolate chips. Nobody seems to mind!

○ ○

gingersnaps

I can't claim to be the genius who developed the glorious spice combination that is a gingersnap, but I like to think I've put my chewy, health-minded signature on it. This recipe produces a fairly flat, crisp-edged cookie; if you like a cakier cookie, add an extra ¼ cup flour. See the photograph on page 8.

○   *Makes 36*   ○ ○ ○ ○ ○

¾ CUP COCONUT OIL

⅓ CUP HOMEMADE APPLESAUCE (PAGE 78) OR STORE-BOUGHT UNSWEETENED APPLESAUCE

1 TEASPOON SALT

3 TABLESPOONS MOLASSES

2 TABLESPOONS PURE VANILLA EXTRACT

1¼ CUPS EVAPORATED CANE JUICE

2 CUPS BOB'S RED MILL GLUTEN-FREE ALL-PURPOSE FLOUR

¼ CUP FLAX MEAL

2 TEASPOONS GROUND CINNAMON

1 TABLESPOON GROUND GINGER

1 TEASPOON BAKING SODA

1½ TEASPOONS XANTHAN GUM

Preheat the oven to 325°F. Line 2 baking sheets with parchment paper.

In a medium bowl, combine the oil, applesauce, salt, molasses, vanilla, and evaporated cane juice. In another medium bowl, whisk together the flour, flax meal, cinnamon, ginger, baking soda, and xanthan gum. Using a rubber spatula, carefully add the dry ingredients to the wet mixture and stir until a grainy dough is formed.

Using a melon baller, scoop the dough onto the prepared baking sheets, spacing the portions 1 inch apart. Gently press each with the heel of your hand to help them spread. Bake the cookies on the center rack for 15 minutes, rotating the sheets 180 degrees after 9 minutes. The finished cookies will be crisp on the edges and soft in the center.

Let the cookies stand on the sheets for 10 minutes, then transfer them to a wire rack and cool completely. Store the cookies in an airtight container at room temperature for up to 3 days.

chocolate chip cookies / cookie sandwiches

In my house, baking cookies was a cutthroat competition among the siblings, with my mother presiding, Iron Chef style, with one baby perched on her hip and another clamped to her knee. Our approaches varied. Mary increased the sugar in an attempt to up the crunch. Patrick (ever the psycho perfectionist) altered the recipe and portion size teaspoon by teaspoon in pursuit of a product with Mom's thin and crispy edges. Bill made his backwards, just to act rad. It was never my intention to upstage your cookies, Mom—but you should know I've never claimed a victory as great as when you tasted your first BabyCakes NYC cookie and said: "These are better than mine." Slather an extremely generous dollop of your favorite frosting (pages 91–95) between two of these cookies and you've got your newest addiction, the BabyCakes NYC cookie sandwich. Try freezing them.

o o o o o o o o o o o o o o o o o o o o o o o o o o o o o o o o o o o o o o o o o o o o o o o o *Makes 36* o o o o

1 CUP COCONUT OIL

6 TABLESPOONS HOMEMADE APPLESAUCE (PAGE 78) OR STORE-BOUGHT UNSWEETENED APPLESAUCE

1 TEASPOON SALT

2 TABLESPOONS PURE VANILLA EXTRACT

1¼ CUPS EVAPORATED CANE JUICE

2 CUPS BOB'S RED MILL GLUTEN-FREE ALL-PURPOSE BAKING FLOUR

¼ CUP FLAX MEAL

1 TEASPOON BAKING SODA

1½ TEASPOONS XANTHAN GUM

1 CUP VEGAN CHOCOLATE CHIPS

Preheat the oven to 325°F. Line 2 baking sheets with parchment paper.

In a medium bowl, mix together the oil, applesauce, salt, vanilla, and evaporated cane juice. In another medium bowl, whisk together the flour, flax meal, baking soda, and xanthan gum. Using a rubber spatula, carefully add the dry ingredients to the wet mixture and stir until a grainy dough is formed. Gently fold in the chocolate chips just until they are evenly distributed throughout the dough.

Using a melon baller, scoop the dough onto the prepared baking sheets, spacing the portions 1 inch apart. Gently press each with the heel of your hand to help them spread. Bake the cookies on the center rack for 15 minutes, rotating the sheets 180 degrees after 9 minutes. The finished cookies will be crisp on the edges and soft in the center.

Let the cookies stand on the sheets for 10 minutes, then transfer them to a wire rack and cool completely before covering. Store the cookies in an airtight container at room temperature for up to 3 days.

double chocolate chip cookies

Have you been eating twice as much chocolate now that studies have shown *conclusively* that this miraculous bean is actually good for you? It's certainly more appealing than gulping down a $7 wheatgrass shot with the rest of the aerobics squad at the health-food store. Here, then, is BabyCakes NYC's ode to cocoa: A tried-and-true chocolate-worshiping recipe with crunchy edges and a soft, chewy center that will put you in antioxidant overdrive. Bonus tip: If you add minced fresh mint to the dough, the cookies taste just like Girl Scout Thin Mints! So here's to putting those overachieving little nerdlettes out of business. (Oh, relax. Love, *love* you gals!)

o o o o o o o o o o o o o o o o o o o o o o o o o o o o o o o o o o o o o o *Makes 36* o o o o o

1 CUP COCONUT OIL

1¼ CUPS EVAPORATED CANE JUICE

⅓ CUP HOMEMADE APPLESAUCE (PAGE 78) OR STORE-BOUGHT UNSWEETENED APPLESAUCE

½ CUP UNSWEETENED COCOA POWDER

1 TEASPOON SALT

2 TABLESPOONS PURE VANILLA EXTRACT

1½ CUPS BOB'S RED MILL GLUTEN-FREE ALL-PURPOSE BAKING FLOUR

¼ CUP FLAX MEAL

1 TEASPOON BAKING SODA

1½ TEASPOONS XANTHAN GUM

1 CUP VEGAN CHOCOLATE CHIPS

Preheat the oven to 325°F. Line 2 baking sheets with parchment paper.

In a medium bowl, mix together the oil, evaporated cane juice, applesauce, cocoa powder, salt, and vanilla. In another medium bowl, whisk together the flour, flax meal, baking soda, and xanthan gum. Using a rubber spatula, carefully add the dry ingredients to the wet mixture and combine until a dough is formed. Gently fold in the chocolate chips just until they are evenly distributed throughout the dough.

Using a melon baller, scoop the dough onto the prepared baking sheets, spacing the portions 1 inch apart. Gently press each with the heel of your hand to help them spread. Bake the cookies on the center rack for 14 minutes, rotating the sheets 180 degrees after 9 minutes. The finished cookies will be crisp on the edges and soft in the center.

Let the cookies stand on the sheets for 10 minutes, then transfer them to a wire rack and cool completely before covering. Store the cookies in an airtight container at room temperature for up to 3 days.

Storing **Cookies** and **Brownies**

Though I've scaled down my commercial-yield recipes
for this book, it's hard to devise a formula for six
cookies or three brownies, and most of these recipes
do produce a generous quantity. Because not everyone
is trying to feed a family of fourteen (or stock a bakery
for a day's worth of customers), some of you will be
blessed with leftovers. Here are a few storage tips:

To freeze unbaked cookie dough, form the
cookies and flatten them with the heel of your hand
before placing in an airtight freezer container
(cookies will not flatten as well during baking once
the dough has been frozen). Make sure to separate
the layers with either parchment paper or foil to
prevent sticking. When ready to bake, arrange the
cookies on a parchment-lined baking sheet and
defrost on the counter for 2 hours before baking.
You can freeze unbaked dough for up to 2 weeks.

If you plan to eat your baked cookies within
3 days, cover them tightly in plastic wrap and place
in an airtight container at room temperature. To
preserve for up to 1 month, freeze as directed
above.

Brownies and blondies: Both regular and agave
brownies freeze well as long as they are wrapped
well in plastic or sealed in a plastic container. Some
customers prefer the brownies frozen because they
become more fudgelike. As with cookies, you can
reheat brownies and blondies to melt the chocolate
and soften the crumb.

sugarplum cookies

I grew up in California just inches from the Mexican border, so I've always had an affinity for that country's culture—in particular the lightly spiced cookies rolled in powdered sugar and served at weddings, ingeniously referred to stateside as Mexican Wedding Cookies. My homage to this perennial favorite has more crunch and some newfangled flavors, but I'm sure you'll agree it, too, is piñata-worthy.

○   Makes 36   ○ ○ ○ ○

¾ CUP PLUS 2 TABLESPOONS
COCONUT OIL

1¼ CUPS EVAPORATED CANE JUICE

½ CUP HOMEMADE APPLESAUCE
(PAGE 78) OR STORE-BOUGHT
UNSWEETENED APPLESAUCE

1 TEASPOON SALT

2 TABLESPOONS PURE VANILLA EXTRACT

2 CUPS BROWN RICE FLOUR

¼ CUP FLAX MEAL

1 TEASPOON BAKING SODA

1½ TEASPOONS XANTHAN GUM

1 TABLESPOON GROUND CINNAMON

½ TEASPOON GROUND NUTMEG

½ CUP CONFECTIONERS' SUGAR

PLUM JAM (I LIKE ST. DALFOUR BRAND)

Preheat the oven to 325°F. Line 2 baking sheets with parchment paper.

In a medium bowl, mix the oil, evaporated cane juice, applesauce, salt, and vanilla until fully combined. Add the flour, flax meal, baking soda, xanthan gum, cinnamon, and nutmeg directly to the wet ingredients, and combine until a dough is formed. If it crumbles, add cold water, 1 tablespoon at a time, until the dough comes together in a ball.

Using a melon baller, scoop the dough onto the prepared baking sheets, spacing the portions 1 inch apart. Press your thumb into the center of each ball to make an indentation. Bake the cookies on the center rack for 16 minutes, rotating the sheets 180 degrees after 8 minutes. The finished cookies will be golden and firm to the touch.

Let the cookies stand on the sheets for 10 minutes, then transfer them to a wire rack and cool completely. Pour the confectioners' sugar into a shallow bowl and roll the cookies through it until completely coated. Spoon 1 teaspoon plum jam into each indentation. Store the cookies in an airtight container at room temperature for up to 3 days.

volcanoes

As you know, it's easy to get overwhelmed in the kitchen, and often the smartest thing you can do is delegate responsibilities. Trust me when I tell you it is perfectly safe to farm out this recipe to some antsy houseguests or eager, enterprising children. It's virtually infallible and can take on just about any flavor you like, no matter how clumsy the chef. Find the vanilla sauce–filled center too timid? Stir in a tiny bit of beet juice to make it a little more Hollywood.

o o o o o o o o o o o o o o o o o o o o o o o o o o o o o o o o o o o o o o o   *Makes 28*   o o o o

2 CUPS RED VELVET CRUMB BASE
(PAGE 116)
½ CUP VANILLA SAUCE (PAGE 91)
¼ CUP CHOCOLATE SAUCE (PAGE 93)

Preheat the oven to 325°F. Line a baking sheet with parchment paper.

Using a melon baller, scoop the crumb base onto the prepared baking sheet, leaving 1 inch between portions. Press your thumb into the center of each to make a small indentation. Bake the volcanoes on the center rack for 16 minutes, rotating the sheet 180 degrees after 6 minutes. The finished volcanoes will be firm and slightly crunchy to the touch.

Let the volcanoes stand on the sheet for 15 minutes, or until completely cooled. Fill each volcano with vanilla sauce. Fill a squeeze bottle or a small bowl with the chocolate sauce and drizzle some over the tops. Serve right away, or store in an airtight container at room temperature for up to 3 days.

macaroons

Many allergic, health-conscious, and vegan bakers are quick to write off macaroons because two of the three ingredients are sugar and eggs. But with a versatile crumb mixture (pages 115–116) at your disposal, this isn't a problem. Grab your preferred crumb (I like vanilla for this recipe) and get to it. Make sure that when spooned out, your mixture retains its shape on the baking sheet; if it falls apart, it's too dry and you need to add a bit more agave. If it spreads, you've gone overboard with the agave and need to add more crumb. The baked macaroons will be the same size as the uncooked. Because of the intensity of the coconut, I prefer them the size of a melon-ball scoop or even a bit smaller.

Makes 24

1 CUP VANILLA, CHOCOLATE, OR RED VELVET CRUMB BASE (PAGES 115–116)

1 CUP UNSWEETENED SHREDDED COCONUT

¼ CUP AGAVE NECTAR, OR AS NEEDED

½ TEASPOON SALT

Preheat the oven to 325°F. Line a baking sheet with parchment paper.

In a medium bowl, mix together the crumb, coconut, agave nectar, and salt with a rubber spatula. If the mixture does not hold together, add more agave nectar, 1 tablespoon at a time, until the dough holds its shape.

Using a melon baller, scoop the dough onto the prepared baking sheet, leaving ½ inch between portions. Bake the macaroons on the center rack for 20 minutes, rotating the sheet 180 degrees after 10 minutes. The macaroons should be golden brown and firm to the touch.

Let the macaroons stand on the sheet for 20 minutes. Serve warm, or transfer them to a wire rack and cool completely before placing in an airtight container and storing at room temperature for up to 3 days.

brownies

I used to make from-the-box brownies on Friday nights to keep me busy during c

Miami Vice, in my opinion the premiere television drama behind *Degrassi High.* M

taught me that if you take the brownies out of the oven about five minutes early

perfect gooey texture. At BabyCakes NYC, I developed a recipe to replicate that c

a full cooking time, mostly to avoid the retching stomachache I'd have for the second half of the Don

Johnson fashion parade. Initially these brownies were made in a square casserole pan and each batch

yielded twelve brownies. Because they are so rich, however, I decided to bake them in mini-muffin

trays and serve them as bite-size morsels. Now these tiny little flavor agents are nearly impossible

to keep in the case. If you're whipping up a batch, be warned: You may want to double the recipe.

o o o o o o o o o o o o o o o o o o o o o o o o o o o o o o o o o o o o o o o o o   *Makes 36*   o o o o

1 CUP GARBANZO–FAVA BEAN FLOUR

¼ CUP POTATO STARCH

2 TABLESPOONS ARROWROOT

½ CUP UNSWEETENED COCOA POWDER

1 CUP SUGAR

2 TEASPOONS BAKING POWDER

¼ TEASPOON BAKING SODA

¼ TEASPOON XANTHAN GUM

1 TEASPOON SALT

½ CUP COCONUT OIL, PLUS MORE
FOR THE TINS

½ CUP HOMEMADE APPLESAUCE
(PAGE 78) OR UNSWEETENED
STORE-BOUGHT APPLESAUCE

2 TABLESPOONS PURE VANILLA EXTRACT

½ CUP HOT WATER OR COFFEE

1 CUP VEGAN CHOCOLATE CHIPS

Preheat the oven to 325°F. Lightly grease three 12-cup mini-muffin tins with oil.

In a medium bowl, mix together the flour, potato starch, arrowroot, cocoa powder, sugar, baking powder, baking soda, xanthan gum, and salt. Add the ½ cup oil, applesauce, vanilla, and hot water to the dry ingredients and stir until the batter is smooth. Using a rubber spatula, gently fold in the chocolate chips just until they are evenly distributed throughout the batter.

Using a melon baller, scoop the batter into each prepared mini-muffin cup. Bake the brownies on the center rack for 10 minutes, rotating the tray 180 degrees after 5 minutes. (For a fudgier cake, bake for only 8 minutes total.) The finished brownie will have a firm edge with a soft center, and a toothpick inserted in the center will come out clean.

Let the brownies stand in the pans for 10 minutes; they are best served warm. To maintain freshness, leave the brownies in the tins until ready to serve. Cover with plastic wrap and store at room temperature for up to 3 days.

Making **Applesauce** and **Other Purées**

Purées have become the foundation of my cookie and cake recipes. Roasting and breaking down fruits to incorporate into your batters is an ideal way to take your baked creations to the next level—and you'll notice the difference immediately. This simple addition provides hearty flavor, moisture, and can be tailored to your taste with minimal fuss. The recipe that follows applies to any of the fruits (pears, peaches, even pumpkin) included in this book. Simply roast your chosen fruit (see page 27 for more information on roasting fruit) and proceed.

APPLESAUCE

ROASTED APPLES (PAGE 27)
¼ CUP AGAVE NECTAR
1 CUP HOT WATER

Spoon the roasted apples into a food processor or a blender and add the hot water and agave nectar. Blend the apples until they are smooth, about 1 minute.

If you do not plan to use the purée immediately, transfer to an airtight container and store in the refrigerator for up to 1 week.

agave-sweetened brownie gems

In order to get the same melty chocolate sensation that comes with the basic brownie without evaporated cane juice, I rely on a simple method of denting the agave brownies in the center and filling them with a puddle of rich, silky chocolate sauce (page 93). The sauce seeps out when bitten into and is so gratifying I wasn't surprised when they began to move off the shelves faster than their sweeter counterpart. You can mix it up a bit by adding vanilla sauce to the center if there happens to be some, you know, lying around. Be sure to keep a special eye on the agave with this recipe. It'll dictate whether you end up with a dry chocolate roll or a luscious fudgelike brownie.

∘ *Makes 36* ∘ ∘ ∘ ∘

½ CUP GARBANZO–FAVA BEAN FLOUR

¼ CUP BROWN RICE FLOUR

¼ CUP POTATO STARCH

2 TABLESPOONS ARROWROOT

½ CUP UNSWEETENED COCOA POWDER

2 TEASPOONS BAKING POWDER

¼ TEASPOON BAKING SODA

¼ TEASPOON XANTHAN GUM

1 TEASPOON SALT

½ CUP COCONUT OIL, PLUS MORE FOR THE TINS

⅓ CUP AGAVE NECTAR

½ CUP HOMEMADE APPLESAUCE (PAGE 78) OR STORE-BOUGHT UNSWEETENED APPLESAUCE

1 TABLESPOON PURE VANILLA EXTRACT

½ CUP HOT WATER OR HOT COFFEE

CHOCOLATE SAUCE (PAGE 93)

Preheat the oven to 325°F. Lightly grease three 12-cup mini-muffin tins with oil.

In a medium bowl, whisk together the flours, potato starch, arrowroot, cocoa powder, baking powder, baking soda, xanthan gum, and salt. Add the ½ cup oil and the agave nectar, apple-sauce, vanilla, and hot water to the dry ingredients and stir until the batter is smooth.

Using a melon baller, scoop the batter into each prepared mini-muffin cup. Bake the brownies on the center rack for 9 minutes, rotating the tins 180 degrees after 5 minutes. (For a more fudgy-tasting cake, bake for only 8 minutes total.) The finished brownies will have firm edges with a soft center, and a toothpick inserted in the center will come out clean.

Let the brownies stand in the tins for 20 minutes, or until completely cool. While they are still in the tins, press your thumb into the center of each and fill the depression with 1 teaspoon chocolate sauce. To maintain freshness, leave the brownies in the muffin tins until ready to serve. Cover with plastic wrap and store at room temperature for up to 3 days.

blondies

This recipe's dynamic is hard to explain, and I really like that. This is the charm of the blondie. The vanilla and chocolate have a subtle repartee, with neither really dominating nor giving way to the other. Initially, the vanilla seems to cede center stage to the chocolate, but if you pay close attention, you'll notice how the vanilla rounds out the chocolate with a seductive mellowness, ultimately creating balance. Making them bite-size gives a great crunchy texture, but you can also bake them in a cake pan and serve them as squares. Either way, blondies are best served warm.

○   *Makes 36*   ○ ○ ○ ○

½ CUP GARBANZO–FAVA BEAN FLOUR

½ CUP BROWN RICE FLOUR

½ CUP POTATO STARCH

¼ CUP ARROWROOT

1¼ CUPS EVAPORATED CANE JUICE

2 TEASPOONS BAKING POWDER

¼ TEASPOON BAKING SODA

1 TEASPOON XANTHAN GUM

1 TEASPOON SALT

½ CUP COCONUT OIL, PLUS MORE FOR THE TINS

⅓ CUP HOMEMADE APPLESAUCE (PAGE 78) OR STORE-BOUGHT UNSWEETENED APPLESAUCE

2 TABLESPOONS PURE VANILLA EXTRACT

½ CUP HOT WATER

1 CUP VEGAN CHOCOLATE CHIPS

Preheat the oven to 325°F. Lightly grease three 12-cup mini-muffin tins with oil.

In a medium bowl, whisk together the flours, potato starch, arrowroot, evaporated cane juice, baking powder, baking soda, xanthan gum, and salt. Add the ½ cup oil and the applesauce, vanilla, and hot water and stir until the batter is smooth. Using a plastic spatula, gently fold in the chocolate chips just until they are evenly distributed throughout the batter.

Using a melon baller, scoop the batter into each prepared mini-muffin cup. Bake the blondies on the center rack for 9 minutes, rotating the tins 180 degrees after 5 minutes. The finished blondies will be golden brown and firm to the touch.

Let the blondies stand in the tins for 10 minutes. To maintain freshness, leave the blondies in the muffin tins until ready to serve. Cover with plastic wrap and store at room temperature for up to 3 days.

Zooey Deschanel, testify!

BabyCakes is beyond pleased to introduce this gifted and inspirational chanteuse and one of BabyCakes NYC's favorite young actresses! (With great hair, besides!)

I have multiple food sensitivities and am always trying my best to eat in a healthful and conscious way. I'd pretty much given up on the idea that I might be able to have a worthy treat ever again. I was so excited to discover BabyCakes NYC, because not only can I eat everything they bake, it's all delicious! I would first like to say that the chocolate chip cookies are the best I have ever had—and that's including the days when I could eat whatever cookie I wanted. But the chocolate chip blondie and the agave-sweetened brownie are some of the most elegant treats around, and are perfect petit fours for a tea party or a luncheon. They are rich and wonderful without being overpowering—a terrific complement to a favorite tea or a cup of coffee. Plus they are irresistibly cute!

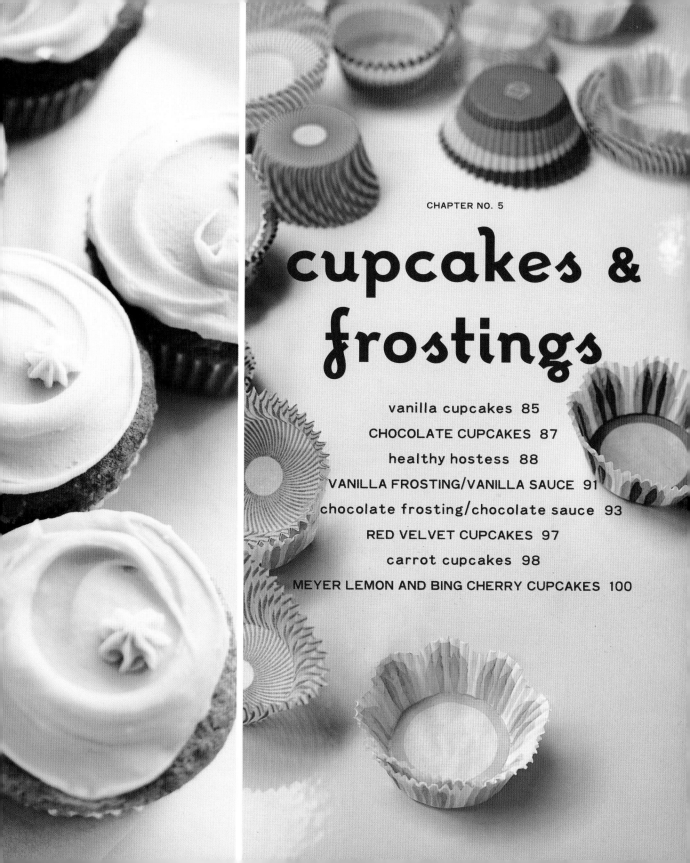

cupcakes & frostings

○ ○

Did you turn to this page directly after scanning the table of contents? After browsing through the photos, did the frosting become a minor obsession? We're not so different, you and I. In your place, I'd probably do the same thing.

Originally, I'd hoped only to make a cupcake I could be proud of, something that people who tragically were forced to go without could indulge in. But the Great Cupcake Craze of 2006 was just dawning, and in a marketplace filled with sensible Easy Spirit pump—like confections, BabyCakes NYC quickly became the field's Christian Louboutin. Long story short, *New York* magazine named mine the best cupcake in New York City—and that's of *all* cupcakes, vegan and otherwise. To my mind, the recognition meant the gap between the allergy—cuffed and the sugar—happy was finally bridged, a true cause for celebration. (And yet another glass of champagne!)

Of course, a cupcake is only as good as its frosting. Before BabyCakes NYC, I hadn't found a frosting that fully met the needs of allergy sufferers and vegans alike—or one that completely dispelled preconceived notions of what a sugar—free anything could be in the best of all possible worlds.

Sure, these recipes make a lot of cupcakes (such is my affection for them). You can halve the recipe if you must, but I would never steer you wrong deliberately. We're friends, remember? Better than anyone, I know this stuff can be expensive and time—consuming, so I'd never condone waste. Au contraire; go ahead with the recipe as directed and reap the benefit of any leftovers to make the precious crumb bases (pages 115–116).

Not a day passes that I'm not asked for the cupcake and frosting recipes. It makes me impossibly happy to share them now.

○ ○

vanilla cupcakes

The recipe that started it all. After five thousand or so failed attempts to produce a vegan, gluten-free cupcake in my slanted, 6-foot-by-5-inch kitchen in Brooklyn—with an oven that flared to broil at whim and had long since lost its temperature dial—I had to tape a picture of a cupcake on the fridge to remember what a cupcake should look like. When I finally hit the right formula, though, I knew it immediately. The cake was delicate and golden, tasting subtly of vanilla with a faint hint of lemon. Now, when I see rows of these beauties on the speed rack at the bakery awaiting frosting, it's hard not to slip into nostalgic reverie.

∘ *Makes 24* ∘ ∘ ∘ ∘

2 CUPS GARBANZO–FAVA BEAN FLOUR

1 CUP POTATO STARCH

½ CUP ARROWROOT

1 TABLESPOON PLUS 1½ TEASPOONS BAKING POWDER

½ TEASPOON BAKING SODA

1 TEASPOON XANTHAN GUM

2 TEASPOONS SALT

⅔ CUP COCONUT OIL

1⅓ CUPS AGAVE NECTAR

¾ CUP HOMEMADE APPLESAUCE (PAGE 78) OR STORE-BOUGHT UNSWEETENED APPLESAUCE

3 TABLESPOONS PURE VANILLA EXTRACT

GRATED ZEST OF 1 LEMON

1 CUP HOT WATER

VANILLA FROSTING (PAGE 91)

Preheat the oven to 325°F. Line 2 standard 12-cup muffin tins with paper liners.

In a medium bowl, whisk together the flour, potato starch, arrowroot, baking powder, baking soda, xanthan gum, and salt. Add the oil, agave nectar, applesauce, vanilla, and lemon zest to the dry ingredients and combine. Stir in the hot water and mix until the batter is smooth.

Pour ⅓ cup batter into each prepared cup, almost filling it. Bake the cupcakes on the center rack for 22 minutes, rotating the tins 180 degrees after 15 minutes. The finished cupcakes will be golden brown and will bounce back when pressure is applied gently to the center.

Let the cupcakes stand in the tins for 20 minutes, then transfer them to a wire rack and cool completely. Using a frosting knife, gently spread 1 tablespoon vanilla frosting over each cupcake. Store the cupcakes in an airtight container in the refrigerator for up to 3 days.

chocolate
cupcakes

If the vanilla cupcake is my doted-on firstborn, the chocolate version is my wild and unruly second child. Prone to petulant deflation, the chocolaty batter forced me to employ every disciplinary technique I could think of before it embraced its chocolate roots and revealed its softer, billowy side. This recipe is not as subtle as the vanilla cupcake; expect a rich, fudgy cake with an intense flavor that resonates with the most feral of chocolate addictions.

o o o o o o o o o o o o o o o o o o o o o o o o o o o o o o o o o o o o o o o o   Makes 24   o o o o

1¾ CUPS GARBANZO–FAVA BEAN FLOUR

½ CUP POTATO STARCH

1 CUP UNSWEETENED COCOA POWDER

¼ CUP ARROWROOT

1 TABLESPOON PLUS 1½ TEASPOONS BAKING POWDER

½ TEASPOON BAKING SODA

½ TEASPOON XANTHAN GUM

2 TEASPOONS SALT

1 CUP COCONUT OIL

1⅓ CUPS AGAVE NECTAR

¾ CUP HOMEMADE APPLESAUCE (PAGE 78) OR STORE-BOUGHT UNSWEETENED APPLESAUCE

3 TABLESPOONS PURE VANILLA EXTRACT

1 CUP HOT WATER OR HOT COFFEE

CHOCOLATE FROSTING (PAGE 93)

Preheat the oven to 325°F. Line 2 standard 12-cup muffin tins with paper liners.

In a medium bowl, whisk together the flour, potato starch, cocoa powder, arrowroot, baking powder, baking soda, xanthan gum, and salt. Add the oil, agave nectar, applesauce, vanilla, and hot water to the dry ingredients. Stir until the batter is smooth.

Pour ⅓ cup batter into each prepared cup, almost filling it. Bake the cupcakes on the center rack for 22 minutes, rotating the tins 180 degrees after 15 minutes. The finished cupcakes will bounce back when pressure is applied gently to the center.

Let the cupcakes stand in the tins for 20 minutes, then transfer them to a wire rack and cool completely. Using a frosting knife, gently spread 1 tablespoon chocolate frosting over each cupcake. Store the cupcakes in an airtight container in the refrigerator for up to 3 days.

healthy hostess

This is my healthy version of the popular Hostess® cupcake. This double-stuffed cupcake is a frosting lover's fantasy (see Anderson, Pamela, opposite). Although the recipe calls for 1 tablespoon frosting for the filling, you won't be blamed for upping the amount a bit—just be reasonable! Too much and you'll bury the innocent, delicious cake. Although I have found what follows to be the best flavor pairing, you can freely use any of the cupcakes and frostings in this book together with dazzling results.

Makes 24

1 CUP BROWN RICE FLOUR

1 CUP GARBANZO–FAVA BEAN FLOUR

1 CUP UNSWEETENED COCOA POWDER

½ CUP POTATO STARCH

¼ CUP ARROWROOT

1 TABLESPOON BAKING POWDER

¾ TEASPOON BAKING SODA

¾ TEASPOON XANTHAN GUM

2 TEASPOONS SALT

1 CUP COCONUT OIL

1½ CUPS AGAVE NECTAR

1 CUP HOMEMADE APPLESAUCE (PAGE 78) OR STORE-BOUGHT UNSWEETENED APPLESAUCE

1 TABLESPOON PURE VANILLA EXTRACT

1 CUP HOT WATER

VANILLA FROSTING (PAGE 91)

CHOCOLATE FROSTING (OPTIONAL, PAGE 93)

Preheat the oven to 325°F. Line 2 standard 12-cup muffin tins with paper liners.

In a medium bowl, whisk together the flours, cocoa powder, potato starch, arrowroot, baking powder, baking soda, xanthan gum, and salt. Add the oil, agave nectar, applesauce, and vanilla to the dry ingredients. Stir until you have a thick batter. Pour in the hot water and continue mixing until the batter is smooth.

Pour $1/3$ cup batter into each prepared cup, almost filling it. Bake the cupcakes on the center rack for 24 minutes, rotating the tins 180 degrees after 14 minutes. The finished cupcakes will bounce back when pressure is applied gently to the center, and a toothpick inserted in the center will come out clean.

Let the cupcakes stand in the tins for 20 minutes, then transfer them to a wire rack and cool completely. Cut each cupcake horizontally in the center. Using a frosting knife, spread 1 tablespoon vanilla frosting on the bottom layer and set the top of the cupcake back on it. Frost the top of the cupcake with another tablespoon of the vanilla frosting. (For an extra-pretty cupcake, fill a pastry bag with chocolate frosting and pipe chocolate curlicues onto each cupcake.) Store the cupcakes in an airtight container in the refrigerator for up to 3 days.

LOVE FROM THE FAN CLUB:
Pamela Anderson

You know her, you love her (me, too!),
and she needs no real introduction . . .
Ladies and gentleman, the pride of
PETA, Ms. Pamela Anderson!

A little-known fact: Animals especially appreciate being rescued by friends in white, French-
cut bikinis as opposed to those in modest onesies
(I don't know why, they just do). And, of course,
I'm happy to oblige—I've long been committed
to sticking up for defenseless animals and the
worldwide proliferation of sexy water-wear. But
to successfully rock a shockingly shocking suit
requires less chubby desserts. Thank all that is
holy for BabyCakes NYC and my new favorite indulgence: the sultry Healthy Hostess (aka
Healthy Ho). In the wrong hands, vegan fare can
be tasteless, boring, and unattractive, but
these are the greatest things since the California sunshine. When I bring the Ho's around my boys
and their buddies, they hover like undernourished
pigeons, and with pals on set or at a fund-raiser
it's the same thing. In the end, I'm happy to pimp
my Ho's around town if it means chickens and
cows remain unharmed and that people are made
to realize that making delicious recipes doesn't
require the use of any animal products.

How to **Color** Frosting **Naturally**

Just because you support fair-trade coffee, drive a hybrid car, and drink wheatgrass every day doesn't mean your cupcakes have to be drab, dull, and devoid of color. Here are a few natural ways to get vibrant colors that will have everyone wondering where you're stashing your Easter egg dye. Because Mother Nature works in mysterious ways, color your frosting no more than a few hours before applying it, as the colors tend to change over time. And because each juice is concentrated differently, be sure to add coloring little by little until you reach the desired hue.

Pink/Red: Cherry, raspberry, cranberry, pomegranate, and beet juice all give gorgeous color.

Purple: Blueberry juice delivers a regal purple—the more you use, the deeper the hue.

Green: Chlorophyll is the green pigment found in most plants. You can find it in liquid form at your local health-food store.

Yellow: Turmeric is a plant in the ginger family that is usually dried and ground into a powder. Just a pinch will tint your frosting the yellow of a freshly opened Peep, and it's completely vegan.

vanilla
frosting/vanilla sauce

Let's just dive in, shall we? Not only does this recipe produce a thick and creamy vanilla frosting, it also doubles as a whipped topping, and left unrefrigerated it becomes a vanilla sauce to serve with crumbs, shortcakes, or volcanoes. And why stop there? I especially love the sauce on savory bites like the corn bread, muffins, and biscuits, where it acts like a decadent sweet butter. If you try to steer clear of soy, replace the liquid and powdered soy with the rice milk variety for both in equal measure—but be advised that the result will taste slightly sweeter. Please note: If it's true frosting you want, be sure to factor in the full 6 hours for it to chill and set.

o o o o o o o o o o o o o o o o o o o o o o o Makes enough to frost 24 cupcakes o o o

1½ CUPS UNSWEETENED SOY MILK
¾ CUP DRY SOY MILK POWDER
1 TABLESPOON COCONUT FLOUR
¼ CUP AGAVE NECTAR
1 TABLESPOON PURE VANILLA EXTRACT
1½ CUPS COCONUT OIL
2 TABLESPOONS FRESH LEMON JUICE

In a blender or a food processor, combine the soy milk, soy powder, coconut flour, agave nectar, and vanilla. Blend the ingredients for 2 minutes. With the machine running, slowly add the oil and lemon juice, alternating between the two until both are fully incorporated. Pour the mixture into an airtight container and refrigerate for 6 hours or for up to 1 month. (If you plan to use it as a sauce, store the mixture at room temperature for up to 1 week.)

chocolate frosting /
chocolate sauce

If there's ever a time to search out a high-end cocoa powder, it's before you dig in and make a batch of chocolate frosting. Invest in some French Valrhona, if at all possible. It has a remarkably rich and excellent flavor. Quick tip: For a more milk chocolaty frosting, replace 2 tablespoons unsweetened cocoa with soy milk powder. For a deep, rich chocolate sauce, add 2 tablespoons agave nectar to the mix and store at room temperature instead of refrigerating.

o o o o o o o o o o o o o o o o o o o o o o o o o o o *Makes enough to frost 24 cupcakes* o o o

1½ CUPS UNSWEETENED SOY MILK

½ CUP DRY SOY MILK POWDER

¼ CUP UNSWEETENED COCOA POWDER

1 TABLESPOON COCONUT FLOUR

¼ CUP AGAVE NECTAR

1 TABLESPOON PURE VANILLA EXTRACT

1 CUP COCONUT OIL

2 TABLESPOONS FRESH LEMON JUICE

In a blender or a food processor, combine the soy milk, soy powder, cocoa powder, coconut flour, agave nectar, and vanilla. Blend the ingredients for 2 minutes. With the machine running, slowly add the oil and lemon juice, alternating between the two until both are fully incorporated. Pour the mixture into an airtight container and refrigerate for 6 hours or for up to 1 month. (If you plan to use it as a sauce, store the mixture at room temperature for up to 1 week.)

How to **Frost** a **Cupcake**

Like all the best things in life, BabyCakes NYC frosting requires careful handling. I was so concerned that each cupcake leaving the bakery be perfect that for a year after opening, I frosted each one personally. After our first hectic holiday season, that practice was tossed out the window, and these days I have a team of frosters who run circles around me with the tricks I've taught them for working with this delicate confection. Now it's your turn. Put on your favorite frosting tunes (Fleetwood Mac works well, or you can buy my brother Frankie's hit song "BabyCakes NYC Wassup" on our website) and get to it.

Prepping Your Frosting

○ Remove the frosting from the refrigerator and stir with a palette knife. If the frosting is too stiff, let it sit at room temperature for 5 minutes or so. Don't let it come to room temperature, though, or it will begin to melt.

○ If the frosting is too soft, add melted coconut oil, 1 tablespoon at a time, until a consistency similar to that of cream cheese or peanut butter is achieved. Because coconut oil becomes solid when chilled, it thickens cold frosting instantly. Cool, right?

Applying Frosting

○ Scoop up a generous tablespoon of frosting with a palette knife or a frosting spatula.

○ Starting at the center of the cupcake and moving outward, spread the frosting in a tight circular motion.

○ Create a waved look by dipping a knife into the frosting and, holding the knife still, spinning the cupcake a full rotation as you pull it away.

Piping Flowers and Designs

○ Chilled frosting can also be piped onto cakes and cupcakes from a pastry bag fitted with the decorative tip of your choice. Please note: The heat of your hands will eventually melt the frosting, so be careful to squeeze from the end of the bag, not the center.

red velvet
cupcakes

Ask someone what, exactly, red velvet is, and chances are they'll stare back at you blankly. Nonetheless, red velvet remains the top-selling cupcake in America ("America" means BabyCakes NYC, of course). As I've come to understand it, the name dates to the time when people carried books with a belt and wore bonnets, and cocoa powder was still all natural and reacted with the acid in buttermilk and baking soda by turning it a reddish brown, an effect some precolonial marketing genius dubbed *red velvet*. You might be sad to hear that, historically, red velvet cake was appreciated primarily for its neutral (you can say it: bland) flavor and supple texture, which served primarily as a vehicle for frosting. While I obviously have nothing against frosting, I believe the cake should be more than a booster seat, so I've gone ahead and fixed that little problem for you. Thank me by baking these by the thousands.

o o o o o o o o o o o o o o o o o o o o o o o o o o o o o o o o   *Makes 24*   o o o o

½ CUP RICE MILK

2 TABLESPOONS APPLE CIDER VINEGAR

3¼ CUPS WHOLE SPELT FLOUR

⅓ CUP UNSWEETENED COCOA POWDER

1 TABLESPOON PLUS 1 TEASPOON BAKING POWDER

½ TEASPOON BAKING SODA

2 TEASPOONS SALT

⅔ CUP COCONUT OIL

1¼ CUPS AGAVE NECTAR

2 TABLESPOONS PURE VANILLA EXTRACT

5 TABLESPOONS NATURAL RED FOOD COLORING, OR AS NEEDED TO ACHIEVE YOUR PREFERRED DEPTH OF COLOR

VANILLA FROSTING (PAGE 91)

Preheat the oven to 325°F. Line 2 standard 12-cup muffin tins with paper liners.

Pour the rice milk and apple cider vinegar into a small bowl, but do not stir; set aside to develop into "buttermilk."

In a medium bowl, whisk together the flour, cocoa powder, baking powder, baking soda, and salt. Add the oil, agave nectar, and vanilla to the dry ingredients and stir to combine. The batter will be thick. Using a plastic spatula, add the "buttermilk" and mix just until combined. Slowly add red food coloring by the tablespoon until the batter is the desired color. Do not exceed 6 tablespoons, as this will make the batter too wet.

Pour ⅓ cup batter into each prepared cup, almost filling it. Bake the cupcakes on the center rack for 24 minutes, rotating the tins 180 degrees after 14 minutes. The finished cupcakes will bounce back slightly when pressed, and a toothpick inserted in the center will come out clean.

Let the cupcakes stand in the tins for 20 minutes, then transfer them to a wire rack and cool completely. Using a frosting knife, gently spread 1 tablespoon vanilla frosting over each cupcake. Store the cupcakes in an airtight container in the refrigerator for up to 3 days.

carrot
cupcakes

My sister Joanne was once a major disciple of Susan Powter, author of the "Stop the Insanity" series and the face that launched a trillion potato recipes. We McKenna girls eagerly adopted her fat-free mantra "One slice of cheese or ten baked potatoes?!" and happily toted Molly McButtered bagels to school each day. We even developed our own carrot muffin that had less than 1 gram of fat. Of course, over time, counting fat grams on the hour tends to *incite* insanity rather than stop it. Today everyone knows that good fats in the right amount are a beneficial part of your diet. This recipe makes no pretense of being fat-free, but it's got all the best stuff in all the right places.

○ **Makes 24** ○ ○ ○ ○ ○

3 CUPS BOB'S RED MILL GLUTEN-FREE ALL-PURPOSE BAKING FLOUR

1 TABLESPOON BAKING POWDER

1 TABLESPOON BAKING SODA

1 TEASPOON XANTHAN GUM

1½ TEASPOONS SALT

1 TABLESPOON GROUND CINNAMON

2 TEASPOONS GROUND GINGER

½ TEASPOON GROUND NUTMEG

⅔ CUP COCONUT OIL

1 CUP AGAVE NECTAR

1 CUP RICE MILK

1 TABLESPOON PURE VANILLA EXTRACT

½ CUP HOT WATER

3 CUPS SHREDDED CARROTS

VANILLA FROSTING (PAGE 91)

Preheat the oven to 325°F. Line 2 standard 12-cup muffin tins with paper liners.

In a medium bowl, whisk together the flour, baking powder, baking soda, xanthan gum, salt, cinnamon, ginger, and nutmeg. Add the oil, agave nectar, rice milk, and vanilla to the dry ingredients and stir until a thick batter is formed. Add the hot water and continue mixing until the batter is smooth. Using a plastic spatula, gently fold in the carrots just until they are evenly distributed throughout batter.

Pour ⅓ cup batter into each prepared cup, almost filling it. Bake the cupcakes on the center rack for 25 minutes, rotating the tins 180 degrees after 14 minutes. The finished cupcakes will bounce back slightly when pressed, and a toothpick inserted in the center will come out clean.

Let the cupcakes stand in the tins for 20 minutes, then transfer them to a wire rack and cool completely. Using a frosting knife, gently spread 1 tablespoon vanilla frosting over each cupcake. Store the cupcakes in an airtight container in the refrigerator for up to 3 days.

Happy **Hour**

Sure, our cupcakes are delicious—maybe even the best in the city—but what our customers are passionate about is the frosting. When I began selling frosted cupcake tops at the bakery, I wasn't trying to be clever. It was just an easier way for people to fast-track the frosting. Eventually I was cutting out the cake altogether and selling paper shot glasses filled with frosting for people to upend in a minute of unimpeded bliss. And thus did the fabled frosting shot come into being. I don't dare go a day without offering them at the bakery for fear I'll be hounded with angry calls and vicious letters, as I was when I briefly took them off the menu. Seriously. Grab yourself a bag of mini paper cups and get to squeezing. But be warned: People will *never* forget.

meyer lemon and
bing cherry cupcakes

All right, pull the Stepford Wife ensemble out of mothballs and apply your signature color lipstick: It's photo time! While the still-life aesthetic of this cupcake is its own reward, I swear on my highlights that the taste surpasses its beauty. Make sure to avoid overchopping your cherry chunks, and try for a nice, thick lemon zest—the added texture pairs neatly with the creamy frosting.

○ *Makes 24* ○ ○ ○ ○

1¾ CUPS AGAVE NECTAR

GRATED ZEST AND JUICE OF 6 MEYER LEMONS

24 FRESH BING CHERRIES, PITTED AND DICED

2 TEASPOONS SALT

½ CUP GARBANZO–FAVA BEAN FLOUR

1½ CUPS BROWN RICE FLOUR

1 CUP POTATO STARCH

½ CUP ARROWROOT

1 TABLESPOON PLUS 1 TEASPOON BAKING POWDER

½ TEASPOON BAKING SODA

1½ TEASPOONS XANTHAM GUM

¾ CUP COCONUT OIL

¾ CUP HOMEMADE APPLESAUCE (PAGE 78) OR STORE-BOUGHT UNSWEETENED APPLESAUCE

1 TABLESPOON PURE VANILLA EXTRACT

1 TABLESPOON PURE LEMON EXTRACT

⅔ CUP HOT WATER

VANILLA FROSTING (PAGE 91)

In a small saucepan, whisk together the agave nectar, lemon zest, and lemon juice. Cook over medium heat until the mixture boils. Reduce the heat and continue to simmer for 10 minutes; set aside.

Place half the cherries in a small mixing bowl and add ¼ cup of the lemon-infused agave nectar and ½ teaspoon of the salt.

Preheat the oven to 325°F. Line 2 standard 12-cup muffin tins with paper liners.

In a medium bowl, whisk together the flours, potato starch, arrowroot, baking powder, baking soda, xanthan gum, and remaining 1½ teaspoons salt. Add the lemon–agave nectar mixture, oil, applesauce, and vanilla and lemon extracts to the dry ingredients. Mix until completely combined. Add the hot water and stir the batter until smooth.

Scoop ¼ cup batter into each prepared baking cup. Spoon 1 teaspoon prepared cherries onto the center of each cupcake, then top with another 1 tablespoon batter. Bake the cupcakes on the center rack for 24 minutes, rotating the tins 180 degrees after 12 minutes. The finished cupcakes will bounce back slightly when pressed, and a toothpick inserted in the center will come out clean.

Let cupcakes stand in the tins for 20 minutes, then transfer them to a rack and cool completely. Using a plastic spatula, gently fold the remaining chopped cherries into the frosting. With a frosting knife, liberally apply the cherry frosting to the top of the cooled cupcakes. Store the cupcakes in an airtight container in the refrigerator for up to 3 days.

cakes & crumbles

o o o o o o o o o o o o o o o o o o o o o o o o o o o o o o o o o o o

the greatest misconception about cakes is that making them requires an event—a birthday, a wedding, a long-awaited divorce. But I'm a firm believer in the idea that a cake *is* the occasion. I promise that if you pull together one of the recipes that follow on any random, run-of-the-mill Tuesday, your roommate, husband, baby, or houseguest will worship you.

Everyone can get involved in making a cake (there's plenty to do) or you can be a possessive, glory-seeking soloist. Remember, though, that some of the best cakes are collaborative efforts, especially if you have a munchkin handy (I'm a huge fan of child-driven art direction). Besides letting them pour in the ingredients and lick the bowl, you present them with what once was a few ingredients in the pantry and is now a towering image of delicious beauty, and above anyone else, they'll be most forthcoming with praise and awe. But mommies, don't be shy about dropping in a half cup or so of port-soaked cherries as a filling on Ladies' Night.

If you are planning a party and are too freaked you'll mangle your manicure the day of, you have my blessing to make the cake a day in advance. I find that the frosting locks in the moisture, so load it on, stash the cake in the fridge, and breathe easy. If you want to freshen the cake's appearance, add a second thin layer of frosting just before setting it out.

So are we ready, then? Are you nervous? Don't be. The recipes in this chapter are incredibly simple and abundantly rewarding. Be sure to have the camera ready. Kodak moments lie dead ahead.

o o o o o o o o o o o o o o o o o o o o o o o o o o o o o o o o o o o

triple-chocolate *fat pants cake*

I'm all for mindful eating—scanning each and every nutritional label, chewing each bite of food twenty times before swallowing—but we all know there comes a time when we want to slide into a pair of elastic-waisted pants and go to town. When that urge arises, I, for one, succumb. Composed of three of the bakery's most popular items—frosting, brownies, and cookies—this extraordinary layered cake is an indulgence that would make even the lovely Paula Deen blush. Right with you, Ms. Deen!

○ *Makes 25 slices* ○ ○ ○

¾ CUP GARBANZO–FAVA BEAN FLOUR

1 CUP BROWN RICE FLOUR

1 CUP UNSWEETENED COCOA POWDER

2 CUPS EVAPORATED CANE JUICE

½ CUP POTATO STARCH

¼ CUP ARROWROOT

1 TABLESPOON BAKING POWDER

¾ TEASPOON BAKING SODA

½ TEASPOON XANTHAN GUM

2 TEASPOONS SALT

1 CUP COCONUT OIL, PLUS MORE FOR THE PANS

1 CUP HOMEMADE APPLESAUCE (PAGE 78) OR STORE-BOUGHT UNSWEETENED APPLESAUCE

2 TABLESPOONS PURE VANILLA EXTRACT

1 CUP HOT WATER OR HOT COFFEE

2 CUPS VEGAN CHOCOLATE CHIPS

VANILLA FROSTING (PAGE 91)

12 CHOCOLATE CHIP COOKIES (PAGE 68)

Preheat the oven to 325°F. Line the bottoms of three 9 x 3-inch round cake pans with circles of parchment paper and coat lightly with oil.

In a medium bowl, whisk together the flours, cocoa powder, evaporated cane juice, potato starch, arrowroot, baking powder, baking soda, xanthan gum, and salt. Add 1 cup oil and the applesauce, vanilla, and hot water to the dry ingredients and stir until the batter is smooth. Using a rubber spatula, gently fold in the chocolate chips just until they are evenly distributed throughout the batter.

Divide the batter evenly among the prepared pans. Bake the cakes on the center rack for 24 minutes, rotating the pans 180 degrees after 12 minutes. The finished cakes will be firm to the touch, and a toothpick inserted in the center will come out clean.

Let the cakes stand in the pans for 20 minutes, then gently run a knife around the edges. Cover the top of each pan with a cutting board and flip over. Carefully lift the pan away and re-invert the cake onto a wire rack to cool completely.

Transfer one layer to a serving plate or a cake stand. Using a frosting spatula, gently spread a thick layer of vanilla frosting over the top of the cake. Break up the cookies and crumble some evenly over the frosting. Place a second layer on top. Repeat the frosting/crumbling process. Set the third layer on top of the second layer and repeat the frosting/crumbling process one last time. Cover the cake with a dome and store in the refrigerator for up to 3 days.

Jason Schwartzman

One of BabyCakes NYC's most steadfast
supporters, this gifted actor and tremendous
friend has been with us since the very beginning.
Welcome, Jason Schwartzman, everyone . . .

It arrived in the mail, a welcome-home gift. I'd just
returned from India filming *Darjeeling Limited* and Erin
knew how badly a snack was needed. In the box I found the
following: a bag of chocolate chip cookies, 2 large round
brownie-cake-like things (I call them "rownies"), and
1 large jar of frosting. A note explained that I had everything I needed to build my very own lo-fi Triple Chocolate
Fat Pants Cake. There were instructions. A small
diagram. There were arrows and many scribbled notes.
Do-it-yourself. Ikea.

But the last thing I wanted to do was build and eat
this epic Fat Pants alone in sad silence. A surprise visit
from my brother Robert suggested the perfect occasion.
His band happened to be playing, and I thought, *After-
party build-a-Fat-Pants shindig?!?!?!*

The band played that night, and they were great. But
honestly, my mind was on The Pants. So many questions. So
many fears.

After the show we went back to my apartment quickly.
The kitchen and tools were located. Layer by layer we built
The Pants, me a nervous surgeon, my girlfriend a mindful
assistant. At last, there she was. A gigantic brownie-
cookie-sandwich thing!

We cut slices. A toast was made, eye contact was
made. And we bit in.

Oh man. The best thing. We ate it so hard. First soft
and cakey and then sweet and cold (the frosting) and then
crunchy and tough and then soft again. It was heaven.
It was Fat Pants. Now every time I see a hot pair of fat
pants, I will think of that magical night. Thanks, Erin, for
the memories.

mint
icebox cake

Dear Outraged Icebox Cake Purist: I understand you will be frustrated and angry that what follows is in no way an icebox cake, and for that I'm sorry. But those traditional icebox cakes you are so staunchly defending are nothing more than raw eggs, butter, and sugar mixed together and dumped into a pit of sponge cake or stale ladyfingers. Not cool for your stomach, or mine! We can do better—and have with this towering ode to the magical pairing of mint and chocolate.

The cake may seem a touch underdone when the baking time is up, but trust me: You will have a beautifully moist cake that won't dry out in the freezer, one you'll pick at happily each time you pass the fridge for weeks to come! If you avoid evaporated cane juice, omit the cookies but add some berries or Chocolate Crumb Base (page 116).

o o o o o o o o o o o o o o o o o o o o o o o o o o o o o o o o o o *Makes 22 slices* o o o o

1¾ CUPS BROWN RICE FLOUR

½ CUP POTATO STARCH

¼ CUP ARROWROOT

1 CUP UNSWEETENED COCOA POWDER

1½ TABLESPOONS BAKING POWDER

½ TEASPOON BAKING SODA

¾ TEASPOON XANTHAN GUM

2 TEASPOONS SALT

1 CUP COCONUT OIL, PLUS MORE FOR THE PANS

1½ CUPS AGAVE NECTAR

½ CUP HOMEMADE APPLESAUCE (PAGE 78) OR STORE-BOUGHT UNSWEETENED APPLESAUCE

½ CUP CANNED SWEET POTATO PURÉE

1 TABLESPOON PURE VANILLA EXTRACT

1 CUP HOT WATER OR HOT COFFEE

3 TABLESPOONS MINT FLAVOR OR PEPPERMINT EXTRACT

VANILLA FROSTING (PAGE 91)

16 DOUBLE CHOCOLATE CHIP COOKIES (PAGE 71)

Preheat the oven to 325°F. Lightly coat three 7 x 4 x 3-inch loaf pans with oil.

In a medium bowl, whisk together the flour, potato starch, arrowroot, cocoa powder, baking powder, baking soda, xanthan gum, and salt. Add 1 cup oil and the agave nectar, applesauce, sweet potato purée, vanilla, hot water, and mint flavor to the dry ingredients and stir until the batter is smooth.

Divide the batter evenly among the prepared pans. Bake the cakes on the center rack for 15 minutes, rotating the pans 180 degrees after 8 minutes. The cakes should feel slightly soft in the center, but firm around the edges.

Let the cakes stand in the pans for 20 minutes, then gently run a knife around the edges. Turn the cake onto a wire rack and cool completely.

Transfer one layer to a serving plate or a cake stand. Using a frosting spatula, gently spread a thick layer of vanilla frosting over the top of the cake. Break up the cookies and crumble some evenly over the frosting. Place a second layer on top and repeat the frosting/crumbling process. Lay the third layer on the second layer and frost the top and sides of the cake completely. Crumble the remaining cookies over the top. Place the cake in the freezer for 2 hours to set the frosting before serving. Store the cake in an airtight container in the freezer for up to 1 month.

double-chocolate crumb cake

By now you've no doubt realized that many of these recipes call for high-quality ingredients that are a bit more costly than a tub of shortening or a sack of bleached flour. As I've mentioned before, though, I also abhor waste. This recipe might be the most ingenious recasting of leftovers you'll ever find, the best part being that nobody could ever possibly know!

o o o o o o o o o o o o o o o o o o o o o o o o o o o o o o o o o o o o o *Makes 8 slices* o o o o

¾ CUP BROWN RICE FLOUR

¼ CUP POTATO STARCH

2 TABLESPOONS ARROWROOT

½ CUP UNSWEETENED COCOA POWDER

2 TEASPOONS BAKING POWDER

¼ TEASPOON BAKING SODA

¼ TEASPOON XANTHAN GUM

1 TEASPOON SALT

½ CUP COCONUT OIL, PLUS MORE FOR THE PAN

⅔ CUP AGAVE NECTAR

⅓ CUP HOMEMADE APPLESAUCE (PAGE 78) OR STORE-BOUGHT UNSWEETENED APPLESAUCE

2 TABLESPOONS PURE VANILLA EXTRACT

⅓ CUP HOT WATER

1 CUP CHOCOLATE CRUMB BASE (PAGE 116)

¼ CUP CHOCOLATE SAUCE (PAGE 93)

Preheat the oven to 325°F. Line the bottom of a 9 x 3-inch round cake pan with a circle of parchment paper and coat both paper and sides lightly with oil.

In a medium bowl, whisk together the flour, potato starch, arrowroot, cocoa powder, baking powder, baking soda, xanthan gum, and salt. Add ½ cup oil and the agave nectar, applesauce, vanilla, and hot water to the dry ingredients and stir until the batter is smooth.

Pour the batter into the prepared pan and bake on the center rack for 20 minutes. Remove the pan from the oven and spoon the Chocolate Crumb over the cake, gently patting it down. Return the pan to the oven and bake the cake for an additional 15 minutes. The finished crumb topping will be slightly crisp to the touch, and the cake will be firm.

Let the cake stand in the pan for 20 minutes, then gently run a knife around the edges. Cover the top of the pan with a cutting board and flip over. Carefully lift the pan away and re-invert the cake onto a serving plate.

Pour the chocolate sauce into a squeeze bottle and drizzle it evenly over the top of the cake in a zigzag pattern from one edge to the other. Rotate the cake 180 degrees and drizzle it again. Cover the cake with a dome and store at room temperature for up to 3 days.

blueberry crumb cake

Before BabyCakes NYC, my dreams were limited to potential hairstyles, sarcastic comebacks, and still more prospective hairstyles. Nowadays, I dream almost exclusively of baked goods. One restless night, after being awakened by images of a fluffy blueberry cake topped with spiced crumbs and a rich vanilla sauce, I sprinted to the bakery to begin testing. I encountered a few setbacks, but once I found out that the crumb cooks faster than the base and must be added halfway through baking, my dream came true. Please don't trust your instincts with this one; the window for applying the crumb is small. Add it too soon and your crumb topping will burn, too late and it will be soggy. Use those timers, people!

○ *Makes 8 slices* ○ ○ ○

1 CUP VANILLA CRUMB BASE (PAGE 115)

3 TEASPOONS GROUND CINNAMON

⅔ CUP BOB'S RED MILL GLUTEN-FREE ALL-PURPOSE BAKING FLOUR

⅓ CUP BROWN RICE FLOUR

1 TEASPOON BAKING POWDER

1 TEASPOON BAKING SODA

¼ TEASPOON XANTHAN GUM

½ TEASPOON SALT

¼ CUP COCONUT OIL, PLUS MORE FOR THE PAN

⅓ CUP AGAVE NECTAR

⅓ CUP RICE MILK

2 TEASPOONS PURE VANILLA EXTRACT

½ TEASPOON PURE LEMON EXTRACT

¼ CUP FRESH BLUEBERRIES

¼ CUP VANILLA SAUCE (PAGE 91)

Preheat the oven to 325°F. Line the bottom of a 9 x 3-inch round cake pan with a circle of parchment paper and coat lightly with oil.

In a medium bowl, combine the vanilla crumb base with 1 teaspoon cinnamon. Set aside.

In a second medium bowl, whisk together the flours, baking powder, baking soda, xanthan gum, salt, and remaining 2 teaspoons cinnamon. Add ¼ cup oil and the agave nectar, rice milk, and vanilla and lemon extracts to the dry ingredients and stir until the batter is smooth. Using a rubber spatula, gently fold in the blueberries just until they are evenly distributed throughout the batter.

Pour the batter into the prepared pan and bake on the center rack for 15 minutes. Remove the pan from the oven and spoon the prepared crumb topping over the cake, gently patting it down. Return the pan to the oven and bake the cake for an additional 15 minutes. The finished crumb topping will be slightly crisp to the touch, and the cake will be firm.

Let the cake stand for 20 minutes, then gently run a knife around the edge. Cover the top of the pan with a cutting board and flip. Carefully lift the pan away and re-invert the cake onto a serving plate.

Pour the vanilla sauce into a squeeze bottle and drizzle it evenly over the top of the cake. Store the cake at room temperature for up to 3 days.

sweet paradise cake

My sister Sarah, the planet's most outrageously particular eater, once told me: "I would rather starve than eat something that isn't a symphony in my mouth." As I would gladly eat a toupee if my blood sugar sank low enough, people like Sarah are like Martians to me. This cake is the perfect bridge between you and the Sarahs in your life. When I finally had the chance to offer her a slice, she took a bite, shut her eyes, raised a finger like a conductor's baton, and began humming Beethoven's Fifth. No joke. I've really become partial to the strawberry filling, but on occasion, at Sarah's request, I substitute both blackberries and blueberries. Stay creative.

o o o o o o o o o o o o o o o o o o o o o o o o o o o o o o o o o o o o *Makes 16 slices* o o o

3½ CUPS WHOLE SPELT FLOUR

1 TABLESPOON BAKING POWDER

¾ TEASPOON BAKING SODA

2 TEASPOONS SALT

1 CUP COCONUT OIL, PLUS MORE FOR THE PANS

1⅓ CUPS AGAVE NECTAR

¾ CUP HOMEMADE APPLESAUCE (PAGE 78) OR STORE-BOUGHT UNSWEETENED APPLESAUCE

3 TABLESPOONS PURE VANILLA EXTRACT

2 CUPS HULLED AND SLICED STRAWBERRIES

VANILLA FROSTING (PAGE 91)

Preheat the oven to 325°F. Line the bottoms of three 8 x 3-inch round cake pans with circles of parchment paper and coat lightly with oil.

In a medium bowl, whisk together the flour, baking powder, baking soda, and salt. Add 1 cup oil and the agave nectar, applesauce, and vanilla directly to the dry ingredients and stir until the batter is smooth.

Pour the batter into the prepared pans. Bake the cakes on the center rack for 22 minutes, rotating the pans 180 degrees after 12 minutes. The finished cakes will be golden brown, and a toothpick inserted in the center will come out clean.

Let the cakes stand in the pans for 20 minutes, then gently run a knife around the edges, cover the top of each pan with a cutting board, and flip over. Carefully lift the pan away and re-invert the cake onto a wire rack to cool completely.

Place one cake layer on a serving plate or a cake stand. With a frosting spatula, gently spread vanilla frosting over the top. Scatter enough strawberries over the frosting to completely cover it. Place a second layer on top, right side up, and spread with more frosting. Add another layer of strawberries. Place the final layer on top, domed side down. Spread the top with frosting and arrange strawberries over it decoratively. Cover the cake with a dome and store in the refrigerator for up to 3 days.

vanilla
crumb base

Did you notice that all my cupcake recipes yield 24? With so many cupcakes (is 24 *really* a lot?), you might, theoretically, have a few left over. Those little leftover treasures are the secret behind my most brilliant invention: the crumb. Crumbs consist of either an unfrosted cake or an unfrosted cupcake broken down and treated with additional flavoring. In most cases, you'll be using cupcakes, which aren't all that sweet on their own and are thus the ideal blank canvas. You'll find the vanilla-based version to be the most versatile crumb of the three I've included. You can add your favorite spices to tailor it to your taste; just don't add more than 2 teaspoons of the spice you choose, or it will overpower the cake you're baking.

○ ○

6 UNFROSTED VANILLA CUPCAKES (PAGE 86)
2 TABLESPOONS COCONUT OIL
¼ CUP AGAVE NECTAR
½ TEASPOON SALT

In a medium bowl, use your hands to crumble the cupcakes into small, fine bits. Add the oil, agave nectar, and salt to the crumb. Using a rubber spatula, fold together the ingredients until thoroughly combined. Store in an airtight container at room temperature for up to 4 days. For longer shelf life, store in the freezer for up to 3 weeks.

chocolate crumb base

Crumbs can function as a binder (Macaroons, page 76), as a toasted topping (Double-Chocolate Crumb Cake, page 110; Blueberry Crumb Cake, page 113), or as a bite-size vehicle for a delicious frosting or sauce (Volcanoes, page 74). The chocolate cupcake contains more oil than its vanilla counterpart, so in the crumb phase you should add less. If you like it on the sweet side, add an additional tablespoon agave nectar, but avoid going beyond that—as is, this recipe packs a massive punch.

○ ○

6 UNFROSTED CHOCOLATE CUPCAKES (PAGE 87)
1 TABLESPOON COCONUT OIL
3 TABLESPOONS AGAVE NECTAR
½ TEASPOON SALT

In a medium bowl, use your hands to crumble the cupcakes into small, fine bits. Add the oil, agave nectar, and salt to the crumb. Using a rubber spatula, fold together the ingredients until thoroughly combined. Store in an airtight container at room temperature for up to 4 days. For longer shelf life, store in the freezer for up to 3 weeks.

red velvet crumb base

I use this version primarily as a base for Volcanoes (page 74), but it could certainly be used for the Double-Chocolate Crumb Cake (page 110) or the Macaroons (page 76), or as a foundation for a special recipe of your own. The red velvet cake, like the chocolate, is already fairly moist and sticky, so it doesn't need much additional oil to hold it together.

○ ○

6 UNFROSTED RED VELVET CUPCAKES (PAGE 97)
1 TABLESPOON COCONUT OIL
¼ CUP AGAVE NECTAR
½ TEASPOON SALT

In a medium bowl, use your hands to crumble the cupcakes into small, fine bits. Add the oil, agave nectar, and salt to the crumb. Using a rubber spatula, fold together the ingredients until thoroughly combined. Store in an airtight container at room temperature for up to 4 days. For longer shelf life, store in the freezer for up to 3 weeks.

The **Big Idea Factory**

Creating your own crumb-based recipe is a great way to exercise your creativity
without putting your dollars at risk. Here are a few ideas to get you rolling:

Create a pie crust: Press a ¼-inch layer of the crumb mixture of your choice into an oiled pie pan. Top with a thin layer of frosting, then a layer of fruit, and freeze for a perfect summer dessert.

Make fudgy truffles: Roll the chocolate crumb mixture into small balls (about 1½ inches in diameter). Dunk the balls in Chocolate Sauce (page 93) and chill for 6 hours before serving. Store in an airtight container in the fridge.

Make old-fashioned rum balls: Add ¼ cup rum (or the liqueur of your choice) and a pinch of cinnamon to the Vanilla Crumb Base (page 115). Roll into 1-inch balls. Bake for 20 minutes at 325°F, roll in confectioners' sugar, and serve.

Decorate cakes: Sprinkle plain crumbs of any flavor on the top and sides of a frosted cake to add a little drama.

pies & cobblers

o o o o o o o o o o o o o o o o o o o o o o o o o o o o o o o o o o o o o o o

there are, traditionally, two schools of pie eaters: the crust lovers and
the filling folk. I know and sympathize with people from each camp and
can say proudly and confidently that I stand smack in the middle—a
peace broker.

Raised on an assortment of Mrs. Smith's pie and the gelatinous filling in
the McDonald's version, I was slow to come around to pie-making. When
it came time to expand the menu at BabyCakes, though, I quickly found
pie-making a Zen-like undertaking. Of course, nirvana is not always
achieved, and mixing up a pie dough that is as charmingly fragile as its filling
is satisfying sometimes makes me downright batty.

Enter cobblers. These are the lowest-maintenance recipes you can find:
Simply fill your baking dish, cover the contents with dough, bake, and scoop
out to serve. To make them a bit more dignified, I've given you an example of
an elegant fruit pairing (blackberry and peach) that can easily be substituted with whatever you prefer.

Not surprisingly, there is unusually high demand for pies and cobblers in the
holiday season, and I expect you'll be turning to these pages then. As trying
as that time of year can be, take comfort in the knowledge that these desserts can be assembled up to 2 days ahead of time, covered in plastic wrap,
and stored in your refrigerator to be baked just as your company arrives.

o o o o o o o o o o o o o o o o o o o o o o o o o o o o o o o o o o o o o

cherry cobbler

Due to the especially juicy and tart nature of cherries, I substitute evaporated cane juice for agave in the cobbler topping for this dessert. It adds a stable texture that can stand up to the cherries. This recipe is for individual-size portions—sometimes (okay, *often*) it's just fine to indulge this type of selfishness.

○ **Makes 8 servings** ○ ○ ○

3 CUPS FRESH CHERRIES, PITTED

¾ CUP AGAVE NECTAR

⅓ CUP ARROWROOT

1 TABLESPOON PURE VANILLA EXTRACT

2 TEASPOONS SALT

2 CUPS WHOLE SPELT FLOUR, PLUS MORE FOR SPRINKLING

1 TABLESPOON BAKING POWDER

⅓ CUP EVAPORATED CANE JUICE, PLUS MORE FOR SPRINKLING

⅓ CUP COCONUT OIL, PLUS MORE FOR THE RAMEKINS

6 TABLESPOONS COLD WATER

In a medium bowl, combine the cherries, agave nectar, arrowroot, vanilla, and 1 teaspoon of the salt. Toss together until the cherries are completely coated.

In a mixing bowl, whisk together the flour, baking powder, evaporated cane juice, and the remaining teaspoon salt. Add the oil and cold water to the dry ingredients and stir to make a dough. If it is too dry, add more water, 1 tablespoon at a time, until a moist, sticky dough is achieved.

Spread plastic wrap on the counter and sprinkle it with spelt flour. Place the dough on the plastic wrap and shape it into a 3-inch-thick flattened disk. Wrap the dough tightly and refrigerate for at least 10 minutes, and up to 3 days, before using.

Preheat the oven to 325°F. Brush eight 6-ounce ramekins with oil and set aside.

Cover your work surface with parchment paper and sprinkle it heavily with spelt flour. Dredge the dough through the flour until it is completely covered. Use a rolling pin to roll the dough out to form a ¼-inch-thick circle about 8 inches in diameter. Use a sharp knife to cut ½-inch-wide strips. Fill the prepared ramekins about three-quarters full with the cherry filling. Arrange the dough strips decoratively over the filling. Brush the strips with oil and sprinkle with evaporated cane juice.

Place the ramekins on a baking sheet. Bake the cobblers on the bottom shelf for 20 minutes, until the crusts are golden and flaky.

Let the cobblers stand for 15 minutes; serve warm. To store leftovers, cool the cobblers completely, then cover with plastic wrap and store at room temperature for up to 3 days.

...ie

...f the most common problems when it comes to baking pies, having the same ...butting too much makeup on a pretty girl. Often, bakers trying to doll up a ...selves left with an overburdened crust and fruit drenched in starchy goo. Have ... selection, and hold back when possible. Here's a recipe that lets each part carry its own weight, leaving your hands free to twiddle thumbs, shoot finger guns, or slap high-fives.

○ **Makes 8 slices** ○ ○ ○ ○

BCNYC Pie Crust

3 CUPS WHOLE SPELT FLOUR, PLUS MORE FOR DUSTING

1 TABLESPOON PLUS ¼ TEASPOON BAKING POWDER

¾ TEASPOON SALT

7 TABLESPOONS COCONUT OIL, PLUS MORE FOR BRUSHING

½ CUP PLUS 2 TABLESPOONS AGAVE NECTAR, PLUS MORE FOR BRUSHING

2 TEASPOONS PURE VANILLA EXTRACT

3 TABLESPOONS COLD WATER

ROASTED APPLES (SEE PAGE 27)

In a medium bowl, whisk together the flour, baking powder, and salt. Add 7 tablespoons oil and the agave nectar and vanilla to the dry ingredients and stir for 20 seconds, or until the dry and wet ingredients are completely combined. Slowly add the cold water to the mixture and continue mixing for an additional 20 seconds, or until a slightly moist dough is formed.

Spread a piece of plastic wrap on the counter and sprinkle it with spelt flour. Dump the dough onto the plastic wrap and shape it into a 3-inch-thick disk. Wrap the dough and refrigerate for 20 minutes before using.

Preheat the oven to 325°F. Line a baking sheet with parchment paper and lightly oil a 9-inch pie pan.

Cover your work surface with parchment paper and sprinkle it heavily with spelt flour. Dredge the dough through the flour until it is completely covered. Using a rolling pin, roll out the dough to an even ¼-inch thickness. Brush off the excess flour. Lift the crust and fit it into the prepared pie pan, allowing the excess dough to hang over the rim.

Fill the pie shell with the roasted apples and spread evenly. Fold the excess dough back over the apples, folding and pleating to create a rustic-looking pie. Brush the dough lightly with oil. Place the pie on the prepared baking sheet and bake on the bottom rack for 20 minutes. Remove the pie from the oven and brush the crust with agave nectar. Return to the oven and bake for 11 minutes longer, until browned.

Let the pie stand for 15 minutes before slicing and serving. Store the pie, covered with plastic wrap, at room temperature for up to 3 days.

ice cream
pie

America's Funniest Pets is, as you know, the greatest reality show on television. And there's no finer accompaniment to a TV night than this incredibly simple, unimaginably delicious pie. If it's possible to make an evening spent watching a dog run around with a bucket on its head more awesome, this pie will get you there. When you try this recipe, take any liberty you can think of to personalize it. You could use any of the cookies in this book for the crust and enjoy fantastic results.

o o o o o o o o o o o o o o o o o o o o o o o o o o o o o o o o o *Makes 8 slices* o o o

16 DOUBLE CHOCOLATE CHIP COOKIES (PAGE 71)

2 TABLESPOONS COCONUT OIL

¼ CUP AGAVE NECTAR

2 PINTS VEGAN VANILLA ICE CREAM (SEE RESOURCES)

½ CUP CHOCOLATE SAUCE (PAGE 93)

In a food processor, blend together 14 of the cookies, the oil, and the agave nectar. Mix just long enough to grind the cookies. Press the crumbled cookies into the bottom and up the side of a 10-inch pie pan to create the crust. Place the pan in the freezer for 2 hours to firm the crust.

Remove the ice cream from the freezer and let it soften for 20 minutes. Spread the ice cream over the firm crust, smoothing the top. Pour the chocolate sauce into a squeeze bottle and drizzle it over the top of the pie in a zigzag pattern. Crumble the remaining 2 cookies and sprinkle them decoratively over the pie. Return the pie to the freezer for 1 hour to set before serving. Place the pie in an airtight container and store in the freezer for up to 1 month.

, peach,
and oat cobbler

...h recipes like planning a seating chart at a dinner party. It's usually a good idea ...narchist teenage nephews, right? Similarly, in a crumble it's best to avoid ...s, like blackberries and cranberries, in the same bowl. For this recipe, I partner the testy blackberry with a dose of mellow peach, whose sweet charms keep the party on an even keel. Also, blackberries tend to lose their structure under heat, while the peaches—like apples and pears—stay true to form and give your crumble hearty body.

Makes 8 slices

3 CUPS SLICED FRESH PEACHES, SKIN REMAINING

1 CUP FRESH BLACKBERRIES

¼ CUP ARROWROOT

½ CUP AGAVE NECTAR

1½ TEASPOONS SALT

1 CUP WHOLE SPELT FLOUR

⅓ CUP ROLLED OATS

3 TABLESPOONS EVAPORATED CANE JUICE, PLUS MORE FOR SPRINKLING

2 TEASPOONS BAKING POWDER

1 TEASPOON GROUND CINNAMON

¼ CUP COCONUT OIL, PLUS MORE FOR BRUSHING

1 TEASPOON PURE VANILLA EXTRACT

¼ CUP HOT WATER

Preheat the oven to 325°F. Line the bottom of an 8 x 3-inch round cake pan with a circle of parchment paper and coat lightly with oil.

In a small bowl, combine the peaches, blackberries, arrowroot, ¼ cup of the agave nectar, and ¼ teaspoon of the salt with a rubber spatula; set aside. In a medium bowl, whisk together the flour, oats, 3 tablespoons evaporated cane juice, baking powder, cinnamon, and the remaining 1¼ teaspoons salt. Add the oil, the remaining ¼ cup agave nectar, the vanilla, and the hot water to the dry ingredients. Stir until a moist dough is formed.

Using a rubber spatula, spread the peach and blackberry mix evenly in the prepared pan. Drop spoonfuls of the batter over the top of the fruit, but do not spread them. Sprinkle the top with evaporated cane juice.

Bake the cobbler on the center rack for 20 minutes. The finished cobbler will have a golden crust, and the juice from the fruit will bubble up through the gaps in the cobbler topping.

Let the cobbler stand for 15 minutes before serving it warm and directly from the pan. Store leftovers at room temperature, covered in plastic wrap, for up to 3 days.

strawberry-rhubarb pie

Hey, Dad! Remember those surprise outings Team McKenna took to Knott's Berry Farm in the early 1980s? When we piled into the station wagon for a two-hour voyage with one seatbelt stretched over three kids? The trips that got you significantly more amped than they did anyone else? I do. Will you admit now that the real reason for those trips was that you were in thrall to the Knott's Berry Farm restaurant's strawberry-rhubarb pie? Twenty years later I've finally come around, and I now understand the overwhelming allure of this delicious pairing. This one's for you, Dad.

o o o o o o o o o o o o o o o o o o o o o o o o o o o o o o o o o o o o o o o o *Makes 8 slices* o o o

3 CUPS DRIED RHUBARB (½-INCH DICE)

1 CUP HULLED AND SLICED STRAWBERRIES

⅔ CUP AGAVE NECTAR

3 TABLESPOONS ARROWROOT

1 TEASPOON GROUND CINNAMON

½ TEASPOON GROUND GINGER

¼ TEASPOON SALT

WHOLE SPELT FLOUR, FOR DUSTING

BCNYC PIE CRUST (PAGE 122)

COCONUT OIL, FOR THE PAN AND FOR SPRINKLING

AGAVE NECTAR, FOR BRUSHING

Place the rhubarb in a medium bowl with the strawberries, agave nectar, arrowroot, cinnamon, ginger, and salt. Toss to combine.

Spread a piece of plastic wrap on the counter and sprinkle it with spelt flour. Dump the dough onto the plastic wrap and shape into a 3-inch-thick disk. Wrap the dough and refrigerate for 20 minutes before using.

Preheat the oven to 325°F. Line a baking sheet with parchment paper and lightly oil a 9-inch pie pan.

Cover your work surface with parchment paper and sprinkle it heavily with spelt flour. Dredge the dough in the flour until it is completely covered. Using a rolling pin, roll out the dough to an even ¼-inch thickness. Brush off the excess flour. With your hands, lift the crust and fit it into the prepared pie pan, allowing the excess dough to hang over the rim.

Fill the pie shell with the strawberry-rhubarb mixture and spread evenly. Fold the excess dough back over the filling, folding and pleating to create a rustic-looking pie. Brush the dough lightly with oil. Place the pie on the prepared baking sheet and bake on the bottom rack for 20 minutes. Remove the pie from the oven and brush the crust with agave nectar. Return to the oven and bake for an additional 11 minutes. The finished crust will be brown and flaky.

Let the pie stand for 15 minutes before slicing and serving. If it will not be served immediately, allow the pie to cool completely before covering with plastic wrap and storing at room temperature for up to 3 days.

Peace **of** the **Pie**

Forgive me if I assume you've never made a pie with the ingredients called for in these recipes, but the truth is, many of these recipes act in ways you couldn't possibly anticipate. I've messed them up enough to know where the pitfalls lurk. Aren't we lucky to have each other? Here's what I've learned:

○ If you're adapting a conventional berry pie recipe, you'll need to add extra agave and arrowroot to the filling—a good rule of thumb is an additional ¼ cup agave and 2 tablespoons more arrowroot beyond what is called for in the recipe per cup of berries. Cooking berries for a long period tends to make them bitter, and the extra sweetener helps offset this.

○ If you want your apple or pear pie especially dense, slice your fruit thin and layer it evenly rather than tumbling the slices into the crust willy-nilly. The point here is to have a crust that lies directly on top of the fruit, preventing air pockets from forming among the slices of fruit.

○ Once you've formed the pie dough, brush the crust with coconut oil before placing it in the oven, in addition to brushing it after 20 minutes of baking. This will soak up the extra flour and give the crust a buttery texture.

○ Bake the pie on the oven's floor for the first 10 minutes of baking. This will give the pie a flaky bottom.

○ Mind the visual clues. If the crust is beginning to brown well before the cooking time is up, cover it with foil to keep it from burning. Poke holes in the center of the foil to prevent the pie from steaming into a dumpling-like disaster.

○ If you want to get the most out of your pie crust, set aside a small handful before rolling out the dough for your pie and reserve it for fruit tartlets. Roll the additional dough into a large rectangle 3 inches wide. Place 2-tablespoon dots of fruit down the center and fold the dough over lengthwise. Seal between the dots of fruit to create small square personalized tarts. Bake at 350°F on a parchment-lined baking sheet for 15 minutes, rotating the sheet 180 degrees halfway through. Let the tarts rest on the sheet for 10 minutes before transferring them to a wire rack.

CHAPTER NO. 8

drinks

o o o o o o o o o o o o o o o o o o o o o o o o o o o o o o o o o o o o o

the girls who work at the bakery are always looking for creative beverages to share, especially in the brutal summer months. You home bakers will find these recipes are a simple way to have a little fun and in the process learn how to sweeten and enliven your favorite refreshments.

You will have noted by now my devotion to the precious coconut, but when it comes to drinks—and shakes in particular—we sadly part ways. The same qualities that make coconut-based products work well in baking recipes (specifically, the thick texture that whips into a high-peaked frosting) makes them a dud, in my opinion, in drinks, where coconut delivers an overly thick consistency and overpowering flavor. Rice milk and soy milk, on the other hand, are perfect in shakes. They are easier to digest and have a more fluid consistency that won't leave you feeling bloated or overstuffed. Be sure to double-check the label when choosing rice and soy milk, though; many contain gluten, and some, believe it or not, have dairy products. Weird, right? Annoying, too.

One last thing: Invest in a good blender. Trust me here. The money you'll save on headache medicine makes it worth each and every penny.

o o o o o o o o o o o o o o o o o o o o o o o o o o o o o o o o o o o o

agave lemonade

Inspired by my daily "free lemonade" that I used to make at the old KFC in grade school, here's a recipe so simple and refreshing that you'll be shocked there are only four ingredients!

○ **Makes 6 servings** ○ ○ ○ ○

14 LEMONS
4½ CUPS FILTERED WATER
¾ CUP AGAVE NECTAR
5 CUPS ICE

Wash 12 of the lemons and cut in half. Juice these lemon halves using an electric juicer.

Fill 6 glasses three-quarters full of ice and set aside. Slice the remaining 2 lemons lengthwise and set aside. In a large pitcher, combine the lemon juice, water, and agave nectar and stir until fully combined. Pour the lemonade over ice, garnish with lemon wedges, and serve.

babyberry

Until the newest wave of mega-size frozen yogurt franchises catch on to the fact that even those of us who can't have dairy would still like a frosty, probiotic-packed soft-serve now and then, we'll just have to make do. And by "making do" I mean blending a chilled masterpiece that will have all the teenyboppers banging down your door for a taste. Tell them to take a number.

○ **Makes 2 servings** ○ ○ ○ ○

**12 OUNCES RICE YOGURT
(I LOVE RICERA BRAND'S BLUEBERRY)**
8 ICE CUBES
½ PEACH, CUT IN CHUNKS

In a blender, combine the rice yogurt, ice, and peach pieces. Blend until creamy. If the mixture is too thin, add more fruit until you reach the desired consistency.

vanilla shake

I'm sure it would be nice to summer in the Hamptons or spend weekends bronzing poolside on the rooftop of a trendy hotel in Manhattan, but the fact is there's baking to be done. To banish the summertime blues, we at the bakery take turns whipping up our own interpretations of the classic vanilla shake. Use the recipe below as the basis for your own adventures in milk shake mixology. My favorite rendition came about when Kylie, part of the bakery's prized counter staff, added a piece of chocolate crumb to the mix and created the most amazing brownie shake in the history of frozen beverages. (Thanks, Kylie!) You can do her one better by adding chocolate chip cookies, fresh mint, or—gasp!—a slice of apple pie.

o o o o o o o o o o o o o o o o o o o o o o o o o o o o o o o o o o *Makes 4 servings* o o o o

1 PINT VEGAN VANILLA ICE CREAM (SEE RESOURCES)

1 CUP UNSWEETENED SOY MILK

¼ CUP AGAVE NECTAR

1 CUP ICE

In a blender, combine the ice cream, soy milk, agave nectar, and ice. Blend for 1 minute. Pour the shake into 4 tall glasses and serve immediately.

Blender Bender

Are you too calorie-conscious even to contemplate an ice cream indulgence? Please don't be like that. Shakes can be great, and they need not live up to their bad rep. Here are a few simple tricks for tailoring the basic vanilla shake to special needs.

Add nutrients. For a shake you can feel good about, toss in ¼ cup flax meal, 2 tablespoons gluten-free oats, and a pinch of cinnamon. This will up the omega-3 and fiber content, and at the same time make the shake hearty enough to stand in for a missed meal.

Trim the fat. To make a low(er)-fat shake, reduce the amount of ice cream by half, double the ice, and add 1 cup banana, which will replace the creamy texture of the missing ice cream. If you dislike banana (oh, I know the sort!), cut the ice cream as before, and add frozen cubes of soy milk in place of the plain ice cubes.

Boost texture, increase deliciousness. If there are any leftover brownies or cookies lying around (it could happen, I suppose), add a handful of crumbles and indulge in a shake that'll change the world as you currently know it.

arnold palmer

If ever we cross paths, there's a 99 percent chance you'll find me sipping a yerba mate tea. The South American beverage quickly became part of my routine once I discovered that it lifts my energy level without the highs and lows of coffee. Come summer, I ice it, stir in some Agave Lemonade (page 133), and relax with the day's saving grace: the BabyCakes NYC version of an Arnold Palmer. If you're confined to the kitchen and have a blender handy, toss in the ingredients, add ice, pulse for a minute or so, and sip your way through the afternoon.

Makes 5 servings

4 YERBA MATE TEA BAGS
2 CUPS ICE
3 CUPS AGAVE LEMONADE (PAGE 133)
5 LEMON WEDGES

Bring a kettle of water to just before the boiling point. Place the tea bags in a teapot and pour 2 cups of the hot water over them. Allow the tea to steep until it is lukewarm; remove the tea bags. Fill 5 glasses halfway with the ice, then top off with the lemonade and yerba mate. Garnish each glass with a lemon wedge.

hot chocolate

I find that soy milk most closely mimics the creamy consistency and richness of traditional hot chocolate, but I know some people don't care for its nutty flavor. If you fall into that camp, rice milk or oat milk will yield equally delicious results. If you choose to substitute either of these alternatives, though, use just 3 tablespoons agave nectar, or your hot chocolate will be far too sweet.

Makes 4 servings

4 CUPS UNSWEETENED SOY MILK
4 TABLESPOONS AGAVE NECTAR
2 TABLESPOONS PURE VANILLA EXTRACT
8 TABLESPOONS UNSWEETENED COCOA POWDER

In a medium saucepan, combine the soy milk, agave nectar, and vanilla. Over a medium flame, heat the mixture for 3 minutes, or until hot. Stir the cocoa powder into the hot milk. Evenly distribute the hot chocolate among 4 mugs.

resources

○ ○

What follows is a small list of brand name products that I use exclusively. With each, I find I'm provided the highest-quality ingredients available, and I believe you'll agree. For additional ingredients and where to find them, please refer to "Purveyors" (page 140), which provides a list of online destinations that will direct you to the ingredients you'll need to make the recipes in this book.

BOB'S RED MILL GLUTEN-FREE
ALL-PURPOSE FLOUR
www.bobsredmill.com

Based in Portland, Oregon, Bob's Red Mill produces a line of organic, gluten-free grains and flours using quartz millstones that deliver an extremely fine flour. Bob's gluten-free all-purpose baking flour and coconut flour are essential ingredients for the recipes included in this book; he also makes garbanzo–fava bean flour, potato starch, arrowroot, rice flour, and spelt flour.

OMEGA NUTRITION COCONUT OIL
www.omeganutrition.com

After trying nearly every available brand of coconut oil, I fell in love with Omega Nutrition, which has become a key ingredient at the bakery. The company uses a patented process that protects the coconut oil's nutrient-rich essential fatty acids from excessive heat, light, and oxygen during production. You can taste the love that goes into this oil, and you'll be absolutely shocked at how closely it mocks the taste and texture of butter.

ORGANIC NECTARS AGAVE NECTAR
www.organicnectars.com

Because baked goods are only as good as the agave used, I knew I had to be incredibly particular about which agave nectar I chose. Organic

Nectars is a company with high standards for quality and a commitment to environmentally conscious practice, which is why their agave nectar ranks above the rest. Their amber-hued syrup adds a mild sweetness that is a perfect complement to BabyCakes NYC's recipes.

GLUTEN-FREE OATS
www.glutenfreeoats.com

Oats aren't considered gluten-free solely because of their proximity to wheat fields. Which is just a terrible thing, in my opinion. A few companies, however, have undertaken the critical and herculean task of producing certified gluten-free oats, and they deserve a huge hug. Gluten-Free Oats is a small company run by a family who counts three generations of celiacs among their ranks. They have a compassionate and firsthand understanding of living gluten-free, and the importance of our partnership with them cannot be overstated.

TEMPTATION ICE CREAM
www.welovesoy.com

When the bakery opened, the founder of Temptation Ice Cream came in and introduced himself. Needless to say, it was session of mutual congratulations, each of us taking turns noting how well the other creates such delicious products without the aid of dairy, eggs, and

○ ○

animal by-products. Their ice cream is so smooth and sweet that most nonvegans I know are truly shocked when told of its sensitive nature. BabyCakes NYC is proud to use Temptation for all our ice cream needs.

INDIA TREE
www.indiatree.com

India Tree offers a chic and varied line of sprinkles and food coloring made with natural colorings and which contain absolutely no trans fats. They are a wonderfully conscientious company, and their products are worth every penny.

SINGING DOG
www.singingdogvanilla.com

You have to love a company that puts the environment first and then goes the extra yard by recirculating a portion of their revenues back to their partner farmers to support organic growing methods. Does this compassion make the best vanilla on the market? By BabyCakes NYC's admittedly high standards, absolutely.

∘ ∘

purveyors

While you may well find all the ingredients in this cookbook at your local health-food store, sometimes it's more convenient to order online—and there are often discounts to be had! Here are a few reliable resources to get your pantry stocked.

WWW.GLUTENFREEMALL.COM

WWW.VEGANSTORE.COM

WWW.ETHICALPLANET.COM

WWW.GLUTENFREE.COM

WWW.GLUTENFREE-SUPERMARKET.COM

WWW.WHOLEFOODSMARKET.COM

WWW.HENRYSMARKETS.COM

WWW.KINGARTHURFLOUR.COM

acknowledgments

○ ○

I was fortunate to have been handed a spatula and the keys to the family pantry early in life, but what I've learned over the years has come slowly and with the help of compassionate, dedicated friends, family, and coworkers whose hearts are as committed as mine.

Thank you . . .

To my family, who continue to shape me and have always been my best cheerleaders. Kathy for the "stalker wall" in your kitchen of all my press you made in my honor; Suzi (and the Stukas family) for your financial vote of confidence; Bill for the spirit-lifting diamonds when I was about to give up; The Official Frank J. for endless BabyCakes NYC original tunes; Mary for writing to Oprah when I had but a single recipe to my name; Danny for being so pro and showing me the ropes; Joanne for teaching me the power of a good comeback; Patrick for explaining that no measuring spoon can be too small; Bridget for pouring all of your spare energy and love into the bakery; Sarah for explaining that it only matters what I think; and Elizabeth for your bright smile, integrity, and loveliness—this book never would have happened without your hard work. Mom and Dad, thank you so much for having me—I love you both.

To my editor at Clarkson Potter, Pam Krauss, to whom I offer my undying gratitude for rolling her wise dice, providing sage advice, and stepping in to save me from myself when I most needed it. Similar acknowledgment must be made of my agent, Carla Glasser, for having the impeccable timing to walk into the bakery on the only day I was crazy enough to think I could find time to write this book. And to Aliza Fogelson, for all your expert finishing touches.

To the invaluable and often overlooked Sabrina Wells, my chief of New York operations, who with her background of having worked in every kitchen from San Francisco to London is a constant source of experience, skill, and support. Without her knowledge of what keeps a kitchen spinning, BabyCakes NYC would be a brilliantly coiffed circus sideshow.

To Krista Marino, for knowing when to slip on Paris Hilton's latest CD to ease me out of a brewing Saturday meltdown.

To all the BabyCakes NYC investors who laid their dollars on the line when the bakery was still just an idea: Mom, Frankie McKenna, Joanne Corvino, Michael Cirelli, Elliot and Ria Van Buskirk, Dana and Michael Beck, Stephanie Escajeda, Phil Tse, and Suzi Stukas. You deserve so much more than I can offer in this small space.

To those who made this book so very, very gorgeous: Tara Donne for capturing the best parts of what we do, and Andrew Camp for assisting her so excellently; Scott Horne for the expert prop styling; Sarah Rappolt of Bumble and Bumble for making all the girls' hair shockingly fabulous; Scott Morrisson and Sharon Weitz from Earnest Sewn and Wendy Mullen and Sameena Ahmad from Built by Wendy for the incredible uniforms.

To all my special guests who so graciously contributed testimonials without hesitation: Mary-Louise Parker, Natalie Portman, Zooey Deschanel, Jason Schwartzman, Pamela Anderson, and Elizabeth McKenna. Each of you—I am your biggest fan. Call me!

To all the bakery staff who have baked and frosted us to where we are today. Never leave me, please.

To you, too, Sister Mary Daniel, because I miss you!

And to Chris Cechin, who almost sent me to the mental institution while we were cowriting this book. Thank you with all my heart for putting so very much into this book's success and for setting the bar so high. I love you.

index

○ ○